The World of Nasrudin

The World
of Nasrudin

Idries Shah

The Octagon Press Ltd
London

Contents

Acknowledgment

The author wishes to express his sincere gratitude to those who have assisted in the preparation of *The World of Nasrudin*.

A Better Beard than Yours

'All true devotees wear a beard,' said the Imam to his audience. 'Show me a thick and lustrous beard and I'll show you a true believer!'

'My goat has a beard far bushier and longer than yours,' replied Nasrudin. 'Does that mean he is a better Muslim than you?'

A Certain Clientele

'*I* have just had an extraordinary dream,' Nasrudin told his wife one morning. 'I dreamt that I met a merchant with four separate loads.'

'What did he have in his saddle-bags?'

'In the first he had persecution and in the second, fear. In the third, intolerance, and in the fourth, blindness.'

'And who were his clients?' asked his wife, intrigued.

'Oppressors, tyrants, Imams, and magistrates.'

A

A Cobbler with Wings

When the Imam saw Nasrudin's scuffed and torn slippers he patted him kindly on the arm: 'Do not despair, Mulla. The Qur'an tells us that he who is needy in this world will be rewarded in Paradise. Your shoes may be worn and holed here, but you shall wear only the best in Heaven.'

'In that case,' replied Nasrudin, 'I will certainly be a cobbler in Heaven.'

A

A Gift from God

Nasrudin was out walking when a bee stung him on the nose. The wound began to swell alarmingly and he hurried off to see the doctor. As he crossed the bazaar, a wag pointed and laughed:

'Where did you get that nose — from a donkey?'

'Yes,' replied the Mulla. 'When God divided the ass, he gave you the brains and me the nose.'

A

A Gift from Tamerlane

To celebrate his birthday, Tamerlane presented each of his courtiers with a large box. As the advisers and nobility opened their presents, they found robes stitched with golden thread and set with precious gems. But when Nasrudin, who had recently fallen from royal favour, unwrapped his gift he found an old donkey blanket inside.

'Merciful Allah,' he cried, 'witness the generosity of Tamerlane, who has honoured his servant with the coat off his own back.'

A

A Happy Childhood

While Nasrudin's neighbour was off trading in a far-away land, he asked the Mulla to look after his three-storey house. Some days later, a strange family moved in, and claimed the property as their own. Nasrudin took them to court.

'How can you be sure the house belongs to your neighbour?' asked the judge.

'Your Honour, I have known the house since childhood, when it was a tiny hut. Think of all the care and attention my neighbour gave for it to grow up to be such a property.'

A

A Humble Target

*I*n Nasrudin's village there lived several delinquent young lads. One day, the Mulla was passing a gang of these youths when their leader threw a stone at his donkey. Instead of punishing the boy, Nasrudin called him over and gave him a meat pie.

'What's this?' sneered the youth, snatching and devouring the pie. 'Trying to tame me with kindness?'

'Nothing of the sort,' replied the Mulla, 'I was simply making up for the fact that you only had my humble donkey as a target. A mischief-maker of your calibre deserves a far nobler mark.'

Wishing to show off in front of his friends, the lad looked about for a more elaborate target. At that moment, the mayor rode by on an elegant stallion. At once, the lad picked up the biggest rock he could find and hurled it at the horse, which shied and threw its eminent rider.

The irate mayor immediately summoned his bodyguards to take the young ruffian away and give him a sound beating.

A

A Loaf for the Head

*N*asrudin arrived at his brother's house late one night and was immediately shown to the best room. Although he was given the most comfortable bed in the house, with the softest sheets and blankets, no one thought to ask if he had eaten. Tossing and turning, Nasrudin struggled in vain to suppress the rumbles of hunger. Finally, he leapt out of bed and called out to his host.

'What is the matter?' asked the Mulla's brother, alarmed at having been woken in the middle of the night.

'The pillows are too soft,' replied Nasrudin. 'Perhaps I could take a loaf from the kitchen and rest my head on that instead?'

A Matter of Opinion

A neighbour's herd of goats got into Nasrudin's garden and hungrily began to devour every bit of vegetation in sight.

'Hurry!' howled Nasrudin's wife. 'Chase those animals away — they are the greediest creatures in the world and will leave us with nothing.'

'Wait a minute,' replied the Mulla, seeing the local Imam coming up the path, 'the greediest of all creatures has not yet arrived.'

A

A Matter of Weight

*N*asrudin had been appointed as the town's judge. Two men came to him with a civil dispute. Some years previously they had bought a donkey. The richer of the two had paid ten gold pieces, the poorer man only five. They had then set up a business collecting firewood which they sold door to door. The man who had invested ten gold pieces in the donkey took a double share of the profits. One day, as they were returning from a town in the mountains, the animal lost its footing and fell over a cliff.

'I paid twice as much for the donkey,' the first owner told Nasrudin, 'and am therefore entitled to some of my money back.'

'I will not give him a penny,' said the second man. 'For several years he has taken twice as much of the profit as I.'

'When the donkey fell, was it carrying a load?' asked the judge.

'No, we were returning from a day's work, having sold the wood.'

'Then it is quite clear,' replied Nasrudin. 'The donkey's fall was directly related to its weight. Therefore, the man who owned the larger share of its body weight was most responsible for its fall.'

He then ordered the first man to pay the second five gold pieces.

A

A Perfect Copy

asrudin was in Turkey visiting a friend. One night, the two men sat outside under the stars. Soon the Mulla stopped talking and started making noises of approval.

'Why do you ooh and ah?'

'I was just admiring your sky, and wondering at the mastery of your sky-painters. They have made a perfect copy of the stars we have back home.'

A

A Pious Man

One day, an Imam called the people of Nasrudin's village together and delivered a sermon on the great deeds of the prophets. As he described the particularly noble achievements of one of these great men, Nasrudin suddenly burst into tears.

'Look at this pious man!' thundered the Imam. 'He is so moved that he weeps.'

'It's true,' sobbed the Mulla, 'you do reduce me to tears. My favourite goat died this morning and I miss him terribly. When you shake your head as you talk, your beard reminds me of my dead goat and I am moved to tears.'

A

A Question of Nature

*O*ne day, the Shah of Iran summoned the greatest thinkers and philosophers of the land to answer a riddle:

'Which came first, the river or the boat?'

'The boat, Your Majesty,' said one, 'for when it was invented, man realised that it could not sail on dry land and had to invent water.'

Nasrudin, who happened to be visiting the Shah's Court, begged leave to ask a second question:

'If fish swim all day, what do they do at night?'

Try as they might, none of the philosophers and sages could find a convincing answer, and Nasrudin finally offered an explanation:

'After a hard day's swimming, the fish are tired so they climb up into the trees and fall asleep.'

'Ridiculous!' clamoured the wise men.

'Why so?' asked Nasrudin. 'Do you think that fish are cattle that they cannot climb trees?'

A

A Question of Timing

asrudin was summoned by the King to advise him on medical matters.

'Tell me,' he asked, 'at what hour is it wisest to dine?'

Nasrudin thought for a moment: 'That all depends on who you are,' he said at last. 'If you are the King, then any time is a good time to dine. If you are a pauper, you eat when you find food.'

A Supper of Oh and Ah

*N*asrudin had no money, and was forced to take temporary employment as a cook.

'Listen, Mulla,' said the gatekeeper on his second day, 'our master is renowned for never paying his servants. Rest assured that the day you ask for your wages, he will set you an impossible task and refuse to pay you when you fail to carry it out.'

Sure enough, the miserly employer withheld Nasrudin's wages for several weeks. Finally, the cook had no choice but to ask his master for the money.

'I will gladly give you your salary,' said the miser when Nasrudin approached him, 'but first, you must cook me a special meal.'

'And what is this meal to consist of?'

'For starters it should consist of "Oh", and for main course it should consist of "Ah",' replied the miser with a smile. 'If you fail to bring me such a meal, I will have no choice but to dismiss you and send you on your way without a penny.'

Nasrudin bowed low and went straight to the kitchen. Some hours later, he emerged and announced that dinner was served. When the miser saw a huge bowl of soup on the table he was delighted. Not only had Nasrudin cooked a savoury meal, but he was about to save several weeks'

A

wages. Taking a large spoonful, he swallowed.

'Oh!' he gasped as the chillies burnt his throat. Spluttering and choking, he extended his arm to the cook, who, in turn, offered him a glass of iced water.

'Ah!' he wept as the cool liquid doused the flames in his mouth.

A Way with Words

gang of burglars, awaiting trial, were worried by the severe sentences being handed out in court. 'We need a man to represent us so eloquently that no judge could convict us,' said their leader. Remembering Nasrudin's way with words, he engaged him as their lawyer.

The Mulla appeared in court the next day and delivered a defence so convincing that all in the court-house were sure that the men were innocent. Nasrudin had put so much energy into his performance that he started to sweat. Seconds before the judge ordered the release of the defendants, their counsel could stand the heat no longer. Removing his coat, he asked the guards to lock it in a cell.

'Why do you want your coat locked up?' asked the judge.

'If these men are to be set free,' replied the Mulla, 'I want to make sure my coat is in a safe place.'

A

A Weaker Man

Walking past an elegant mansion in the heart of the city of Baghdad, Nasrudin heard a party in progress inside. Enticed by the smell of roast goat, he slipped past the guards into the house, and took his place at the table. After the feast his host called for silence.

'Friends,' he declared, 'I have asked you here to celebrate my latest great victories. As you know, I have been the champion wrestler of this city for some time. But having annihilated the competition throughout the land, I am now champion of the entire country!'

The diners started to cheer their host. Only Nasrudin remained silent. This infuriated the wrestler:

'Are you not impressed that I have pulverized my enemies and ground into the dust the best wrestlers this land has to offer?' he demanded.

'That depends,' replied the Mulla. 'Were these other men weaker than you?'

'Of course!' ranted the sportsman. 'They were as feeble as flies... as insignificant as the tiniest ants!'

'What victory is there in defeating a weaker man?'

A Wolf for the Imam

*T*imes were hard, and Nasrudin resolved to find a regular job. Attracted by the easy money, he decided to become an Imam. Wrapping an immense turban around his head, he went in search of a mosque. Many towns and houses of worship later, he had still had no luck. Even the most remote areas turned out to have an Imam already in residence.

Tired and hungry, Nasrudin stopped at a teahouse in a small town at the foot of the mountains. In the square opposite, an angry mob had gathered. Upon investigation, the Mulla discovered that the rabble had trapped a wolf.

'The animal has been attacking our goats and has caused a lot of damage,' one farmer explained. 'By chasing it into town we have finally managed to corner it. We're just discussing what to do with it now.'

Nasrudin unravelled his turban, arranged it on the head of the trapped animal and set it free.

'What have you done?' shouted the amazed onlookers. 'It has taken days to catch it!'

'I have sentenced it to punishment of the worst kind,' replied the Mulla. 'Let it suffer the torment of trying to find work dressed as an Imam.'

A

After your Demise

The Caliph of Baghdad dreamt that his teeth would fall out and his head would lose its hair. In the morning, he summoned the Court astrologer to interpret the dream.

'Alas,' explained the man, 'it means that your wife and children will live on after your demise.'

Hearing this, the enraged ruler had the astrologer thrown in jail.

'How would you interpret the dream?' he asked the Mulla, who was visiting the Court.

'Your Eminence,' replied Nasrudin, 'the dream means that you will outlive your entire family.'

Reassured, the Caliph handed Nasrudin a purse of gold.

A

Allah's Guest

As Nasrudin and his wife were sitting down to supper one night, someone pounded on their door. Opening it, Nasrudin saw a dervish wearing a highly-coloured coat and spotless turban.

'Don't just stand there!' snapped the man, 'I am the guest of Allah himself, and you are obliged to invite me in and provide your tastiest food and drink. Then I shall rest my head on your best pillow and sleep under your warmest blankets!'

'Just a minute,' said the Mulla, struggling into his coat, 'I will take you to a place far more suitable for a holy man such as yourself.' Asking the dervish to follow, he hurried to the town mosque.

'I cannot stay here!' said the indignant sage. 'It is cold and dark and there is nothing to eat.'

'Excuse me,' replied Nasrudin, 'but you said you were Allah's guest and so I naturally assumed that you would be most at home in Allah's house.'

A

Allah's Mercy

asrudin hired a porter to carry his acquisitions home from market. As the two men were climbing the rocky slope to his door, the porter slipped and rolled down the mountainside, screaming.

'Thank you, Allah, for your mercy!' Nasrudin called out, stretching his arms heavenwards.

'How can you thank Allah for allowing a man fall to his death?' asked his wife, who had seen the horrifying accident.

'I am not thanking him for killing the porter: I am thanking him for the fact that I had not paid the unfortunate man. If I had, my money would have joined my groceries at the bottom of the ravine.'

A

Allah's Words

The Shah of Iran heard that Nasrudin, a saint, was travelling through the land. He sent his scouts to locate the blessed one and bring him to live in splendour at Court.

After several months, the Shah visited Nasrudin's luxurious apartments in the palace.

'Tell me, O revered saint, what utterances have you heard from the lips of Allah?'

'Only the last will be of interest to you, Highness. Allah has just whispered in my ear.'

'What does He say?'

'He just told me to watch what I say so that I may remain in the Paradise He has found for me.'

A

Altered Circumstances

Nasrudin and a rich merchant were riding together through the desert.

'Is it not so that God rewards riches with riches?' said the merchant to the Mulla. 'Look at my ravishing riding boots made with the best leather money can buy, and your holed and tattered sandals. Look at my jewelled turban, and the rags you wear wrapped around your head. Look at my silk coat with handcrafted buttons and gold thread, and the patched cloak that hangs from your bony shoulders. Here we two are: you with a few measly possessions in your moth-eaten saddle-bags, I with spices that will make princes and kings weep with pleasure. And yet, we can ride together through this place, I on an Arab stallion, you scrabbling in the sand on a silly little donkey...'

At that moment the merchant's musings were interrupted by the arrival of a band of robbers, who yanked him from the saddle, kicked and beat him to the ground and rode off with his cargo and mount.

'How extraordinary it is,' mused Nasrudin, 'that my circumstances have not seemed to change, but yours are dramatically altered in the space of a few minutes.'

A

Always too Late

Nasrudin had just returned home from the bazaar when he heard the sound of a wedding banquet going on next door. Frantically shedding his work clothes, he washed and, changing into his best robes, flew to his neighbour's house. But in the time it had taken him to change, the feast had finished, the couple had retired for the night and the merrymakers had all set off home.

Returning to his own house, Nasrudin dejectedly started to remove his robes. 'It seems that the first wedding feast I will get to will be my own.'

A

Among Strangers

News came to Nasrudin's village that the judge had died while trying a case in the neighbouring settlement.

'How extraordinary, that he should choose to drop dead in front of complete strangers,' mused the Mulla, 'when he could have done so here among those on his own side.'

Another Man's Treasure

Nasrudin was walking along the riverbank when he saw a goblet floating in the water. Scooping it up, he looked inside, and found that it was half-filled with water. On the surface shimmered a man's face.

'I'm sorry,' he said to his reflection, 'I did not realise that the goblet was yours,' and he hastily returned it to the river.

A

Appetite

One day, Nasrudin's father-in-law — a man with a very large appetite — arrived at the Mulla's house. 'My travels take me right past your house, so I thought I would look in for a few minutes,' he said, taking his place at the table.

Nasrudin served his guest tea and cakes. In a few moments, the man had drunk the last drop and eaten the last crumb of the snack and had begun looking around for more. Nasrudin served more tea and more cakes, and again his father-in-law ate every last morsel and drank every last drop. Ordering his wife to start cooking a pulao of immense proportions, Nasrudin rushed off to fetch sufficient refreshments to sustain their guest until supper. He returned with a huge watermelon, ice-cream, hot pies and nuts, which the man consumed at once.

When the pulao was ready, he ate until there was not a grain of rice left. He then drank six more pots of tea and announced that he would spend the night and continue his journey in the morning. As he settled down in the couple's bed, Nasrudin asked where he was going the next day.

'I am on my way to Samarkand, to see a famous physician who has invented a potion to encourage the appetite. On my way back, I will call in to see you and discuss my adventures.'

A

'What a pity that we will both be away!' cried Nasrudin. 'Tomorrow we leave for Baghdad, to see another famous doctor who has invented a potion to suppress the appetite.'

A

Apples

ulla Nasrudin was once employed as an apple-picker. After a whole day of back-breaking work, his boss — a miser — refused to pay the agreed salary.

'I have no money to offer you, but come back tomorrow and do another day's work and you may eat as many apples as you like.'

The Mulla returned the next day and went on diligently picking fruit from the trees. At sunset he climbed the tallest tree and began to eat apples with such relish that the miser became alarmed.

'Why not eat from the lower branches?' he shouted from the ground.

'I'm starting from the top and working my way down,' called Nasrudin. 'With almost a whole orchard of apples to eat, I'll need to be systematic.'

A

Apricot Rewards

One day, a rabble of mischievous school children watched Nasrudin buy a kilo of apricots in the bazaar. Following him home in the hope of stealing the fruit, they saw him offer an apricot to a man who greeted him on the path. 'This is our chance,' thought the naughty urchins, and they raced ahead via a short-cut. One by one, they approached Nasrudin with greetings and a deep bow. Each boy was given a piece of fruit.

When Nasrudin's bag was empty he saw the doctor coming towards him and immediately hid behind a tree. 'Mulla, are you quite well?' asked the concerned physician, seeing him cowering behind the tree.

'Yes,' replied an embarrassed Nasrudin, 'but I have no apricots left!'

A

Are You Me?

Nasrudin was walking in the crowded city of Baghdad when he bumped into another man and they both fell to the ground.

'Excuse me,' he asked politely, picking himself up, 'are you you, or are you me? Because if you are me, then I must be you.'

'Whoever you are, you are a complete lunatic,' replied the other man when he heard the Mulla's question.

'It is just that you and I are of a similar build and are wearing similar clothes. I thought we might have become muddled in the fall.'

A

Asking the Wrong Man

Nasrudin was trying to fix the chicken coop before the birds had a chance to escape, when he was interrupted by a neighbour.

'How many days are there in a year?'

'Do I look like a year-trader,' snapped Nasrudin, 'that you think that I keep count of the days?'

A

Ask Our Neighbour

One night Nasrudin had a dream that he was married to his neighbour's beautiful young wife. She was so alluring that he could not help but clasp her in his arms and kiss her. But no sooner had he done this than he was woken by a sharp slap.

Blinking the sleep from his eyes, he saw his own, hatchet-faced wife.

'What do you think you are doing?'

'I think you had better ask our neighbour.'

A

Ask Them, not Me

A man greedy for enlightenment came to see Nasrudin.

'I have heard that you are a respected sage. What happens in the next world?'

Pointing to the graveyard, Nasrudin replied:

'I suggest you ask someone over there.'

Ask the Owner

*N*asrudin was walking home when he found a stray goat and decided to lead it to his field. 'That is a splendid goat, Mulla. How much was it?' asked his neighbour.

'A piece of gold.'

'That is a fine goat,' said his wife. 'How much did it cost?'

'Two pieces of gold.'

'That is a nice goat, father,' said his son. 'Was it expensive?'

'Why does everyone keep asking me?' asked Nasrudin. 'Why don't they ask the man who owns it?'

A

Ask your Wife

During the summer months Nasrudin took to sleeping on the roof as it was cooler than his bedroom. One night he was kept awake by his wife's nagging.

'You are a lazy man!' she complained. 'I could have taken my pick of any man in town, but I had to choose a simpleton like you!'

After several minutes of abuse, Nasrudin could stand it no more. He struggled out of bed, but forgot he was on the roof and fell down to the ground. Hearing the crash, his neighbour rushed to investigate.

'How did you get down there?' he asked, seeing the Mulla in a heap on the ground.

'Ask your wife,' replied Nasrudin.

A

Avoidance

Nasrudin's neighbour was always fretting and complaining.

'What shall I do?' he bawled. 'When I get up in the morning, it's so dark that I might bump into something and hurt my foot.'

'Get up an hour later,' suggested the Mulla.

A

Beastly Insults

Nasrudin and his wife were squabbling. Hearing a donkey braying in the street, his wife said: 'There is your father calling you. Go and see what he wants.'

Without a word Nasrudin went outside, and came back a few minutes later.

'He asked me to tell you that your mother, the crow, sends her love.'

B

Being an Expert

group of townswomen were gossiping in the market-square

'My husband always thinks he knows it all,' complained one.

'He certainly can't be more of a know-it-all than mine,' said another.

'Neither of them thinks himself such an all-round expert as my husband,' said Nasrudin's wife.

Just then, Nasrudin saw his wife and came to join the conversation. 'What is the subject under discussion?' he asked.

'Baking,' replied the women, not wanting to admit that they had been complaining about their husbands.

'Ah,' announced Nasrudin, 'I happen to be the most expert baker of cakes in town!'

His wife exchanged a look with her companions. 'Tell us, husband, what ingredients would you choose?'

'Well, it can be tricky because it all depends on the ingredients one has. I usually find that if there is butter, there are no eggs. If there are eggs, there is no butter. If there are eggs and butter, there is no flour or sugar. And if all of the ingredients are present, then I myself am not.'

B

Best Way to Learn

*D*uring a period of particular lawlessness in the country, the King banned the carrying of weapons on the streets. Fearful of being attacked while on his way home one night, Nasrudin concealed a large club beneath his cloak. The weapon was discovered when he was stopped and searched by the police, who took him off to answer to the King.

'Before I throw you in jail, what do you have to say in your defence?' asked the monarch.

'I am a teacher at the local school,' replied Nasrudin, 'and I need the club in order to discipline my pupils.'

'Isn't that a little severe?'

'It may seem so to you, Sire, but you haven't heard the rubbish they come out with.'

Better Be a Sinner

'You are all worthless sinners and layabouts of low moral worth!' a travelling preacher stormed at a collection of villagers. 'Not one man from this place will see the gates of Paradise!'

'Are you sure?' asked Mulla Nasrudin in surprise.

Infuriated at having his words questioned, the preacher turned on the Mulla.

'You may joke all you like, you upstart!' he bellowed, 'but you will be the first to feel the flames of Hell licking at your boots!'

'And where will you be going after your death?'

'Need you ask? A virtuous believer such as myself will go straight to eternal Paradise.'

'In that case,' replied Nasrudin calmly, 'I think it is best if I accompany my friends and kinsmen to Hell. I'd rather tell jokes for their amusement than have to put up with maniacs such as yourself for all eternity.'

Better Bundles

'Quick,' whispered Nasrudin's wife one night, 'there are burglars in the house. I can see the bundles they have left in the garden.' Nasrudin threw back the covers and started to climb out of the window.

'Where are you going?' asked his wife.

'While they are looking through our worthless possessions, I am going to steal their bundles.'

Better off Barefoot

asrudin bought a new pair of shoes and decided to wear them home. He had not gone far when the left shoe started to rub. The Mulla sat and removed the shoe, which rolled down the verge and into a stream. Watching it floating away, Nasrudin looked at the right shoe.

'To tell the truth, I am quite relieved to see your friend go. He was giving me the most terrible blister. Now I can walk home barefoot and you can rest until your friend returns.'

B

Birth and Death

One day, the King summoned Nasrudin to answer a question:

'Tell me, Mulla, for how much longer will babies continue to be born and people continue to die?'

'Birth and death will continue until the fires of Hell have burnt themselves out and Paradise is too full to receive another.'

Bitten Noses

Nasrudin heard his two children fighting outside and went to break them up. In the garden, he found the younger clutching his nose and crying.

'Why are you crying?'

'He bit my nose!' the child whimpered, pointing to his brother.

'That's a lie!' chirped the other. 'He bit his own nose.'

Bones and All

One evening the Imam invited Nasrudin to join him for supper. As the men ate the roast mutton, Nasrudin became aware that his host was surreptitiously placing discarded bones onto his plate.

At the end of the meal the Imam sat back and smiled:

'Look what a glutton you are, Mulla. You have picked clean twice as many bones as your host!'

'If I am a glutton,' replied Nasrudin, 'I wonder what word there is for a man who eats his meat, bones and all?'

B

Borrowed Names

Nasrudin arrived at the palace with a chicken. 'Your Majesty,' he announced, bowing low, 'last night I was playing cards and bet on your name to bring me luck. Thanks to you I won this bird, and I am repaying the debt.'

Much pleased by this, the King accepted the bird. Next day, the Mulla appeared in Court with a goat.

'Your Majesty, once again your name has brought me luck and I would like to offer you this goat in return.'

Again, the King accepted the present.

On the third day, Nasrudin arrived in the throne-room with two rough-looking men.

'Last night,' said the Mulla, 'I borrowed your name once again, but unfortunately this time it failed to bring luck and I now owe these two a hundred pieces of gold.'

The King agreed to pay Nasrudin's debts, but told him never to borrow his name again.

Borrowed Pies

*H*ungry, Nasrudin went to the bazaar to sell his last possessions. An unscrupulous merchant took the collection of household items and said: 'Come back for your money tomorrow, as I have none on me at the moment.'

He refused to pay despite Nasrudin's feeble pleas. Staggering home past the market stalls, the Mulla came across a baker's shop. With his last ounce of strength, he grabbed three pies and made off with them. Sitting in an alleyway he quickly ate the pastries.

'Merciful Allah,' he said as he finished the last pie, 'I am not a thief. I have simply borrowed these pies from the baker. As this is the case, please see that the baker's money is taken out of that owed to me by the merchant who borrowed my pots and pans. I dislike being in debt to any man.'

Borrowed Slippers

*N*asrudin was taking an evening stroll when he stumbled over a man lying on the grass, drunk. Rolling him over, he recognised the drunkard to be none other than the judge — a man famous for passing stiff sentences for moral offences. Seeing that the judge was unconscious, Nasrudin removed his ornate slippers and coat and went on his way.

It was only as the judge stumbled home next day that he realised that he had been robbed. Livid, he told the police to search every house until they had found the culprit.

It was not long before Nasrudin was hauled into court.

'Where did you get those slippers and that coat?' demanded the judge.

'I borrowed them from a drunk I found lying in the gutter late last night,' replied the Mulla. 'I have since tried to return them but do not know the identity of the man. You don't happen to know him, do you?'

'Certainly not!' replied the judge, realising that any other answer would ruin his reputation. 'Case dismissed!'

Boy or Girl?

While Nasrudin was in the Court of Tamerlane the Conqueror, word arrived that his wife had given birth.

'What has your wife had this time?' the Ruler of the World asked Nasrudin.

'Unlike Your Majesty, a humble man such as myself will father either a boy or a girl,' replied the Mulla.

'And what do you suppose Emperors such as myself father?' Timur asked with a smile.

'Tyrants, oppressors, dictators, despots… you have no end of choice.'

B

Burglars and the King

One night, thieves broke into Nasrudin's house and stole everything he owned. When, next morning, he awoke and discovered the loss, he rushed straight to the palace.

'Last night, burglars made off with all my belongings, and it falls upon you to compensate me for my loss,' he told the King.

'But I have taken nothing of yours, Mulla,' said the monarch.

'Not directly,' Nasrudin replied, 'but as ruler of this land, you are responsible for all that happens here.'

Camels and Men

'Nasrudin,' asked his neighbour, 'which is more intelligent, a camel or a man?'

'A camel,' replied the Mulla, 'because it carries heavy loads without complaint, but never asks for an additional load. Man, on the other hand, burdened by responsibility, is always choosing to add to his loads.'

Careless Head

Nasrudin was tying his turban when the wind caught the cloth and carried it away.

'What a shame!' lamented his friend. 'That was a beautiful piece of Indian muslin.'

'I should never have trusted my careless head with it. That is the third turban it has lost this week,' said Nasrudin.

Carving Pheasant

At the King's table one evening, Nasrudin was asked to carve the pheasant. Obligingly, he rose and began to serve the other diners. The head he offered to the King saying: 'You are our leader and the head of your family.'

The wings he gave to the Court treasurer: 'Your embezzlement will be discovered and you will soon take flight.'

The feet he gave to the commander of the army with the words: 'You will soon march into battle.'

The neck he gave to the Grand Vizier saying: 'Your own neck will one day be broken by the hangman's noose.'

The rest of the bird he put on his own plate saying: 'What remains is mine because I have carved so well.'

Chains Tomorrow

Nasrudin was walking home with one of his pupils when he saw some thieves breaking into a house. The Mulla walked quickly by.

'Who were those men,' asked the schoolboy, 'that you hurried by so fast?'

'Convicts,' replied Nasrudin.

'But they had no chains.'

'They will get those tomorrow.'

Cheating the Stars

Nasrudin had made quite a name for himself as the town fortune-teller, for his predictions generally came true.

One day, an old woman approached him and asked:

'Where is my eldest son, Bedar, and what is his fortune?'

'He is living in Baghdad,' replied the Mulla, 'and will remain there in good health for many years to come.'

At that moment a caravan of traders arrived in town.

'Does the mother of Bedar live here?' asked one of the camel men. 'I have been asked by her daughter-in-law to report that Bedar is dead and she is now living in India.'

The angry crowd turned on Nasrudin.

'You are a fraud,' they clamoured. 'And your predictions are worthless!'

'My friends,' announced Nasrudin, 'I am not a fraud, but a fool. The constellations indicate that Bedar enjoys good health, but I was a fool to read the fortune of a man who cheats the stars.'

Child Psychology

Nasrudin's wife was in labour, but the midwife was unable to deliver the child. Finally, in desperation, she turned to the Mulla.

'You are meant to be a wise man. Is there anything you can do to help?'

'If only you had asked before!' exclaimed Nasrudin and rushed off to the bazaar. He returned a few minutes later carrying a top, which he started spinning on the floor.

'Have you gone completely mad?' squawked the midwife.

'Have patience,' replied Nasrudin calmly. 'When the child sees the toy he will jump out and play with it!'

C

Choice Meals

Nasrudin was invited to dine at the house of the town miser. But when the time came for the family to eat, the Mulla was dismayed to be served nothing more than a bowl of milk.

'Eat, my friend!' implored the miser. 'Have some yoghurt, some cream, and some cheese, have some rice pudding, some custard and some butter…'

When the Mulla had drained the bowl he made his excuses and returned home hungry.

Next day, he returned the miser's invitation. As soon as his guest arrived, he ushered him to the dining table, placed a cushion behind his back, a knife and fork in his hands, and a bowl in front of him. When the miser looked into the bowl, he saw only water.

'Eat, my friend!' cried Nasrudin. 'Eat your fill of watermelon and soup, eat the fish and the choicest vegetables, rice and sorbet.'

City Doctors

While in the city, Nasrudin collapsed in the street. Luckily, he was directly outside the house of a doctor. As the man examined him the Mulla gasped:

'Notable physician, I have suffered from this illness for quite some time and do not expect a city man such as yourself to find the cure.'

'It is quite simple,' said the doctor, examining the weak man, 'you are fainting away due to starvation. Food is the only medicine you need.'

With this, he ordered rice and meat to be brought for the traveller. Sure enough, Nasrudin found his strength returning.

'You are a genius. You have healed a dying man. My whole village is suffering from the same disease. As soon as I have the energy, I shall return home and tell my friends and neighbours to come to you for similar treatment.'

C

Civil Unrest

Tamerlane, the Ruler of the Universe, was displeased by unrest in a far corner of his empire. Word arrived that in one of the cities of this region, the peasants had revolted and murdered their oppressive landlord.

Tamerlane called his greatest generals to quell the violence at once.

'Take all the infantrymen you need. Take ladders with which to climb the city walls. Take cannons to reduce the place to dust. Take elephants and camels to strike fear into the heart of every man, woman and child.'

'You have forgotten the one weapon which could settle the dispute before the most powerful element of your forces can,' Nasrudin whispered in the royal ear.

'What is that?' Tamerlane asked in anticipation.

'One sensible man who can listen to the complaints of the locals and then take his place as landlord.'

Close to an Idiot

One day, Nasrudin took a seat in the Turkish baths. The steam was so thick that he could not make out the man on his right.

'How dare you!' snarled the King through the steam. 'Sitting next to me in such a familiar way! You must be close to an idiot!'

'Hang on while I measure,' replied Nasrudin, feeling the space between them. 'I'd say about half a foot.'

C

Coats

One winter's day the judge met Nasrudin in the bazaar.

'Extraordinary,' he mused. 'I am wearing the warmest of my fur-lined coats and am still chilled by the wind. While you, dressed in rags, do not appear to feel the cold. How is that?'

'A man who is wearing all his clothes cannot afford to feel the cold,' replied Nasrudin.

Colour Blind

The Shah was very vain indeed. One day, the Court barber remarked that the royal beard was starting to grey, and the unfortunate man was immediately beheaded.

The ruler then looked around for another barber. 'Tell me,' he asked the first candidate, 'do you see any grey hairs in my beard?'

'One or two, Sire,' admitted the man.

'Call the executioner!' ordered the Shah, and he too was led away.

The monarch turned to the next applicant for the job and asked the same question. Horrified by the fate of the last, he bowed low and said: 'Majesty, your noble beard is jet black.'

'Liar,' bellowed the Shah and immediately had the man beheaded.

Finally, he turned to Nasrudin.

'You! How would you describe the colours of my beard?'

'Alas,' said the Mulla, 'I am colour blind.'

C

Come Judgment Day

The whole village had turned out to listen to the teachings of a renowned sage who was touring the country. At the end of the sermon the simple villagers broke into noisy applause. Raising one ring-encrusted hand, the orator signalled for silence:

'My good men and women — on the Day of Judgment go to the banks of the river so that the chaste and the righteous may drink the waters of eternal life, and pass eternity in Paradise.'

'Hang on a minute!' sobbed Nasrudin, who had listened to the sermon with pious tears streaming down his face. 'If only the chaste may taste the holy waters on Judgment Day, how will you or I be able to drink?'

C

Commander of the Hoofed

asrudin was unpopular with the other courtiers, who thought him a favourite of the King.

'Mulla, the King has made you commander of his donkeys,' joked the Grand Vizier one day.

'How honoured I am,' replied Nasrudin. 'Chief of the donkeys must be the best position in the land!'

'How so?' asked the Vizier.

'Because it would put me in charge of you.'

C

Compensation

One day, Nasrudin was called as a witness in a criminal case.

While he was at the court-room, thieves broke into the Mulla's house and stole all his furniture. Returning home to find his possessions gone, Nasrudin headed straight back to the court-room. He piled chairs, tables and benches into a cart and prepared to ride off.

'Do you want to be thrown in jail for the rest of your worthless life?' stormed the irate judge.

'Certainly not, Your Honour,' replied the Mulla, 'I am simply reclaiming what is rightfully mine.'

Confused Sentences

All in the court-room fell silent when they heard the judge sentence a minor offender to fifty lashes. The silence was broken by Nasrudin, who began to howl with laughter.

'Be quiet! Or I shall hold you in contempt of court!' shouted the apoplectic magistrate.

'Forgive me, Your Honour, but you and I both know that the maximum lashes this man can bear is five. I naturally assumed that you had confused your mathematics and multiplied the just sentence by ten.'

C

Console Yourself

The King aimed his arrow at a stag, fired, and missed.

'An unlucky shot, Majesty!' groaned the Grand Vizier.

'A faulty bow, Majesty!' the treasurer simpered.

'Console yourself with the knowledge of how many innocent men you have succeeded in killing, Majesty!' suggested Nasrudin.

Crime and Punishment

While on his travels, Nasrudin entered a particularly devout land. Very soon he was accused of being an infidel. His hands and feet were bound and he was bundled off to stand trial.

The King, a religious fanatic, sentenced the non-believer to fifty lashes.

'What have you to say in your defence before the punishment is carried out?'

'I am no heretic, Sire!' cried Nasrudin. 'You have commanded that I be beaten, but when the Prophet wanted to convert the Arabs to Islam he directed that they be hit with sticks. How is it that I must receive similar punishment for supposedly renouncing Islam?'

Crowded House

Nasrudin and his wife were talking about their parents.

'My mother can cook ever so well,' said the Mulla.

'How can you say that?' shrieked his wife. 'My mother is a hundred times the better cook!'

Seeing red, Nasrudin grabbed the woman by the scruff of her neck and threw her out into the garden.

'What are you doing?' asked his neighbour.

'There is little enough room in the house for two,' explained Nasrudin. 'Four is just too many.'

'Four?'

'Yes, first there was just me and her, then my mother crept in and finally her mother also came to stay. The house was so crammed with them and their pots and pans, that my wife fell out of the door.'

C

Dangerous Glasses

Nasrudin's neighbour started to wear glasses. 'What are they for?' asked the Mulla. 'They magnify,' replied the man.

'Then be careful when you are eating, or your food might grow in size and choke you!' warned Nasrudin.

D

Dangers of Rain

When Nasrudin's first wife died, he remarried. One day, the weather was so bad that he sheltered in the tea-house.

'Just look at the rain!' exclaimed the proprietor. 'I wouldn't be surprised if it washes away the very surface of the ground and all that is below floats up to the top.'

'I hope not,' replied the Mulla, 'for then my last wife would bob up from her grave and chase away her replacement.'

D

Dangers of Sleep

One day, the Court astrologer told the King that he had appeared in his dreams. The Shah immediately had the man tortured until he was prepared to describe the guise his master had taken in the dream.

Hearing the screams of agony, Nasrudin begged permission to leave the palace.

'What causes this impromptu decision to depart?' asked the monarch.

'A knowledge that I do not have control over my subconscious while asleep,' replied the Mulla.

D

Dead Chicken

Nasrudin sold a chicken at the bazaar. The next day the buyer rushed up to his stall. 'You trickster! You sold me a diseased chicken. This morning, it died.'

'How extraordinary,' replied the Mulla. 'It never did that when it was mine.'

Dead or Alive?

Nasrudin met a well-known con-man on the street.

'They told me you were dead and buried!' the Mulla exclaimed.

'As you can see I am alive and quite well,' he replied.

'Don't think I'll fall for that trick,' said Nasrudin. 'If you say you are alive you must be dead, for we all know what a liar you are!'

D

Deceitful Donkey

Nasrudin was riding home from the bazaar daydreaming of the pulao he would have for his supper. With his thoughts full of the saffroned rice, juicy meat and fried onions, he did not pay much attention to the route his donkey was taking home. His daydream was finally broken when the donkey lurched to a halt outside a house.

'Come! I have all the ingredients for your best pulao,' Nasrudin called to his wife. But the woman he saw before him when he eventually looked up, was a complete stranger. Realising that it was not only the wrong wife, but the wrong house and even the wrong village, the Mulla looked at his donkey severely.

'If you had told me that you wish to move here, I would perhaps have considered it, but I will not stand for deceit!'

D

Descendants

For a while, Nasrudin was banished from the King's Court for his constant jibes. Returning to his own village, he started to plant a forest of saplings around his property.

'How you have fallen from royal favour!' chuckled the Imam in glee. 'Your beard will be snow-white before those saplings are a few feet high. And you will certainly never see the trees in their splendour.'

'Show me a man who does not consider his descendants,' replied Nasrudin, 'and I will show you one who is nothing.'

D

Devious Chickens

Nasrudin bought some grain at market and started to dig a pit in which to store it. He dug all day, but the pit seemed to resist going downwards and instead went sideways. Eventually, he dug his way into his neighbour's chicken coop.

'Quick!' he cried to his astounded wife. 'Come and see. I have found some devious chickens under the ground. They have been hiding so that they can steal my grain.'

D

Different Hearts

*N*asrudin was once employed as a cook. One day, his master sent him to the bazaar to buy ingredients for a grand feast to be offered to important guests that night.

Later, when the food was presented, the noble diners were disgusted to find that each dish was made of sheep's heart.

'I told you to prepare a banquet of the utmost delicacies: the sweetest and most pleasant foodstuffs for these honourable guests.'

'Master,' replied Nasrudin, 'what could be sweeter or more pleasant than heart? For it is the organ which holds love, compassion, generosity and mercy.'

Waving this explanation aside, his employer ordered him to return to the kitchen.

'Come back with something decadent and indulgent rather than pure!' he shouted.

One hour passed, then two, and the guests began to fidget with hunger. Eventually the cook reappeared with the replacement food. But to their horror, the plates were once again piled high with sheep's heart. The host and his offended guests demanded an explanation.

'Master,' said the cook, 'this time you asked me to bring

indulgent and decadent dishes of a less pure nature. What could be more indulgent than a heart which seeks to serve only itself? Or more decadent than a heart seeking only pleasure?'

D

Different Owners, Different Birds

Nasrudin was shopping in the bazaar when he saw a peacock being sold for twenty pieces of gold. Rushing home, he grabbed his goose and hastily returned to the bazaar. Here, he set up a stall next to the wealthy merchant in charge of the peacock.

To his amazement, not a single man offered him twenty pieces of gold for his bird, while an interested throng gathered around the trader next to him, bidding vast sums for the ornate bird.

'How is it that you are practically mobbed by customers in their haste to purchase that bird, when my plump goose is left on the shelf?'

'Simple,' replied the merchant, puffing himself up with importance. 'This is a peacock, a bird with ravishing plumage, which preens and struts all day, with head held high. It is as noble as the King!'

'But my goose is just like you!' replied Nasrudin. 'It waddles like you, it hisses like you and it is as filthy as you. Surely you would consider yourself worth twenty pieces of gold?'

D

Different Paths

'You are a great mystic,' said one of Nasrudin's pupils. 'Surely you will know why men take different paths through life instead of all following one true path.'

'Simple,' replied his teacher. 'If everyone followed the same path, we would all end up in the same place, the balance of the world would be tipped, and we would all be thrown into the ocean.'

D

Dissolving Sins

asrudin decided to make his living by absolving the sins of others. He found an old bottle which he half-filled with water. Next he set up a stall in the bazaar. Soon, he had a crowd of people clamouring to be cleansed. Each paid a gold piece and blew into the bottle and was told that their wrong-doings were forgotten. The Conqueror Tamerlane happened to be passing and, noticing the throng around Nasrudin's stall, he stopped for a closer look.

'How many sins can your bottle hold at a time?' he inquired.

'Only one and then I have to shake it up to dissolve the sin in the holy water.'

Tamerlane handed over a piece of gold, blew into the vessel and then held out another coin. Time after time he blew, and time after time Nasrudin accepted the money and dissolved the sin in the water. After several hours, the Conqueror paused:

'I am quite out of breath; come to my house tomorrow and we'll continue.'

And thus, Nasrudin was ensured a steady income for a considerable time, for Tamerlane had many friends in need of the same service.

D

Diving for Food

asrudin was invited to eat at the house of a man renowned for his miserly ways. When the meal was served, the Mulla found that his bowl contained nothing more than a thin soup. Without a word he started to undress.

'Nasrudin! What are you doing?' asked the surprised miser.

'I am preparing to dive into the soup and see if I cannot find a piece of meat hiding at the bottom.'

D

Do Angels Chase Thieves?

The Imam found Nasrudin sitting in the kitchen with his dog.

'You cursed infidel!' he cried. 'Have you forgotten that the Patriarch Noah divided animals into two categories: the clean and unclean?'

'And into which category does my guard dog fall?'

'Into the category of unclean, of course! Drive the filthy cur out of your house or suffer the wrath of God, who will send His angels to your valueless dwelling!'

'And will God's angels chase away thieves and mind my goats?'

'Lunatic!' replied the Imam. 'Why should the holy angels concern themselves with your trifling needs?'

'Then, at the risk of angering God, I am afraid that I must keep my dog.'

Dog or Ox?

One day, the Emir decided to poke fun at Nasrudin. 'How do you feel, Mulla?' he asked with a smile. 'As fit as an ox,' replied the sage.

'Really? As fit as an ox, eh? Don't you mean a dog?'

'Yes,' Nasrudin replied. 'Now you come to mention it, a dog is a better description.'

'How quickly you change your tune, Mulla.'

'Majesty, when you first asked, I did feel as fit as an ox, but after a few moments of your conversation, I remembered that since Your Highness has graced this country with his rule, my life has been similar to that of a dog.'

D

Doing Things in Reverse

One of Nasrudin's witticisms had annoyed the King to such an extent that he told the executioner to give the Mulla a hundred lashes. On hearing the sentence, Nasrudin removed his shirt and loudly called the Court masseuse.

'It is customary to massage the back after, rather than before the whip has done its work,' said the masseuse.

'True,' replied Nasrudin, 'but after I have suffered the whip, I will be in no fit state to appreciate the massage.'

D

Donkey Astrologer

*N*asrudin was tired of being the Court astrologer. The stress of knowing that any inaccurate prediction might lose him his head persuaded him to look for a successor. One day, he led his donkey up to the monstrous, jewel-encrusted throne.

'Your Majesty, I am unable to continue to read the constellations, as I have found an astrologer far more qualified than I.' With this, he pointed to the donkey.

'How is a filthy donkey more qualified to predict than you?' demanded the King.

'He possesses two fundamental qualities which I do not,' replied Nasrudin. 'Ears ridiculous enough to listen to endless stupid questions, and a voice absurd enough with which to answer.'

D

Donkey Burial

After many years of dedicated service, Nasrudin's donkey died. The Mulla was so upset by the animal's demise that he vowed to give it a decent burial. He wrapped the body in a shroud and, late that night, stole into the graveyard and buried it. The villagers got to hear of this and dragged Nasrudin to court.

'Your Honour,' said the Mulla, 'rather than offend, I have simply carried out the indirect will of God. Before my donkey died, she spoke to me in the language of humans. How could she have the gift of speech if not granted by God?'

'And what did the donkey say when she spoke?' asked the judge.

'She asked me to bury her in the cemetery and pay the court twenty gold pieces.'

The charges were dropped.

D

Donkey King

As the debt-collectors carted away the last of his possessions, Nasrudin got on his donkey and went to see the King. After several days' ride he arrived at the palace gates, travel-worn and hungry.

'What is your business here?' demanded the palace guards.

'I am a ruler!'

Bowing deeply, the guards rushed off to inform the King.

'Your Highness, a ruler has arrived.'

'Bring him to me at once!' said the monarch.

When Nasrudin was shown into the gleaming throne room, the King was taken aback by his ragged appearance.

'You are a ruler?'

'Yes, I am.'

'As ruler of this great kingdom, I rule over the land as far as the eye can see. Excuse me for asking such an indelicate question, but what exactly are you ruler of?'

'Well,' replied the Mulla, 'I was once ruler of The Kingdom of The Apple Orchard. Then I was ruler of The Melon Patch. More recently, I was ruler of My Home. But, now that my enemies have made off with most of my wealth and land, times are hard. These days, I am simply ruler of My Donkey.'

The King smiled.

'You are the ruler of Your Donkey — I the ruler of this entire land. We rulers must stick together.'

D

Donkey-loads

One day, the King and the Crown Prince instructed their coachmen to drive them through the royal parkland. Nasrudin was told to accompany them on foot. As the coach sped through the gardens, Nasrudin jogged and panted alongside. After an hour the horsemen slowed and the Mulla assumed that he was to be given a lift. Instead, the Crown Prince extended one arm and dropped two weighty robes on his head.

'Carry these!' he snapped and gave the signal to move on.

Another hour passed and Nasrudin, almost collapsing from exhaustion, still ran alongside.

Finally, the coach stopped again. This time the King put his head out of the window.

'You must be tired, Mulla,' he said. 'Our robes are so wonderfully stitched with gold and rhinestones, that you are carrying a donkey-load.'

'Actually,' puffed the Mulla, 'I am carrying the load of two donkeys.'

D

Donkey versus Steed

Nasrudin was employed by a local governor, an old man who had recently taken a young and beautiful wife. One day, the governor sent for Nasrudin.

'This morning my wife went to visit her parents in the next town. It is now getting late so I want you to go and fetch her.'

Nasrudin set off, but did not return with his employer's bride for several hours.

'What a fool I was to send a slowcoach on a puny donkey to collect my wife!' said the governor. 'Next time I will dispatch a rider on a racehorse.'

Some days later his wife went to visit her father and mother once again and, remembering Nasrudin's tardiness, the governor dispatched his swiftest horseman to collect his wife.

One day passed, then two, then three, and finally a week later, the rider and the governor's wife returned.

'I owe you an apology, Nasrudin,' conceded the governor. 'Your slow donkey proved to be far faster than my stable's fastest steed.'

'It is not what you send, but who you send,' replied the Mulla.

D

Do Something for Yourself

Nasrudin and his employer, a jeweller, were journeying to Iraq to buy some precious stones. One night, the two men settled down to sleep under the stars. Hardly had Nasrudin had time to close his eyes when the jeweller called out:

'Hurry, man! Stoke up the fire, I feel it is beginning to die down.'

'Impossible,' replied Nasrudin. 'I put a large piece of wood on it moments ago.'

A little later, the merchant called out again: 'Quick! Put out the fire! It will attract thieves who will steal all my valuables.'

'Impossible,' replied Nasrudin. 'The fire burned out several minutes ago.'

A minute passed, and the jeweller bellowed: 'Nasrudin, I am being bitten by mosquitoes. Light the fire again.'

'Listen, master,' snapped Nasrudin. 'I have done as you said twice tonight; surely it is time you lifted a finger yourself!'

D

Each Gets what he Deserves

asrudin was sitting in the market-place one afternoon when he saw a fight break out between three merchants. Going over to investigate, he asked:

'Are you not ashamed to skirmish in the dust in this way?'

The men stopped fighting, straightened their clothes and explained:

'We pooled our money and bought eighteen goats. One of us paid half the price, one of us a third, and the last paid a ninth of the total price. Now that we come to divide the animals, we find that we cannot decide how many we each own. And we do not want to cut up the animals.'

'I could decide this for you,' replied the Mulla, 'but each of you will have to give me a reward.'

'You won't start cutting up our goats?'

'That will not be necessary.'

'Very well,' agreed the merchants, 'you may have a reward if you can solve the problem.'

Lining the men and goats up in front of him, Nasrudin began.

'You,' he said to the first man, 'paid half the price: nine of the goats are yours. 'You,' he told the second man, 'paid a third of the amount: take six goats. You,' he said to the third man, 'are owed two goats for your contribution of one ninth of the sum. Which leaves one goat for me.'

And taking his reward he walked off.

E

Eat then Drink

One day, Nasrudin was at a banquet when he noticed a richly-dressed man stuffing food into his pockets.

'It is for my wife,' explained the thief. 'She couldn't come, so I told her I would bring home some food for her.'

Without a word, Nasrudin opened the man's pocket and poured a pot of tea into it.

'What are you doing?' screamed the miser.

'When your wife has eaten all that,' replied the Mulla, 'she will need something to drink.'

Embarrassed, not Offended

asrudin was suffering from a nasty fever and the doctor, who was a regular guest at the Mulla's table, rushed to attend to him.

'Alas!' he said, having examined his friend. 'There is nothing I can do to save you from death.'

Some time passed, and the Mulla made a full recovery, but he never invited the doctor for supper again. Surprised by Nasrudin's unfriendly manner, the doctor went to his house to ask if he had offended the Mulla in some way.

'I am not offended,' blushed Nasrudin when he saw the doctor. 'I am embarrassed. You gave me your professional advice, but my body decided not to listen to you.'

E

Equal Reward

asrudin and the Court jester were the winners of a competition of wit. The Shah awarded each man a hundred gold pieces as his prize.

'But Majesty,' complained the jester, 'it is not fair that I, a comedian famous throughout the land, should receive an equal reward to a nobody.'

Some weeks passed and, during a second competition, the King was offended by both the jester's and Nasrudin's remarks. He ordered that each man be given twenty strokes of the cane.

'But Majesty,' complained the Mulla, 'is it fair that I, a nobody, should receive an equal reward to a man famous for his wit throughout the land?'

E

Every Last Stitch

Nasrudin's wife was sick of his lack of hygiene. 'Why do you eat and sleep in the same filthy clothes, week after week?' she nagged.

'I once dreamt that I was swimming, and while I was in the water, a thief stole every last stitch of my clothes. Since then, I have vowed never to let them leave my sight.'

E

Evil

Nasrudin's sister was married to a brutal and oafish man. One day, she was complaining about her husband:

'What have I done to deserve such an oppressor as a husband?'

'Nothing,' agreed Nasrudin, 'but one cannot always escape evil.'

E

Exile

$\mathcal{T}$amerlane finally lost his patience. 'Nasrudin, I have tried to welcome you at Court, but you have ceaselessly pestered the Royal Ear with your insolence!' With this, he summoned his torturer and ordered that the disgraced Mulla be rolled in tar, covered in feathers, seated back to front on his donkey and exiled from the city.

'A just sentence,' Nasrudin calmly replied, 'but allow your humble servant to make one final request. Let me select a mount most suited to the punishment.'

Grudgingly, Tamerlane agreed. The Mulla left the Court and returned some hours later. Both King and courtiers gasped when they saw that he was dressed in gorgeous robes, wearing a huge turban, and riding the Emperor's favourite black stallion.

'What is the meaning of this outrage?!' spluttered Tamerlane.

'O Leader of the Damned!' replied the Mulla, 'because I selected my mount first, I had to make certain amendments to the style in which you suggested I leave.'

E

Explanations

*R*iding along a mountain road late one night, Nasrudin saw a band of cut-throats coming towards him. He slid from the saddle and hid under his donkey. The gang leader was surprised to see him cowering under the ass.

'Who is hiding there?'

'Just a little donkey,' whispered the Mulla, trembling with fear.

'But this donkey is male.'

'I know, but when I was born my mother was so horrified by my runtish appearance that she ran off, and ever since my father and I have lived alone.'

E

Extraordinary Accounts

Nasrudin owed the cobbler some money, and did all that he could to avoid the man. One day, the two men finally met on the street.

'Nasrudin! I was beginning to think that you had left town without paying me.'

'Actually I was just on my way to settle up,' replied the Mulla. 'Let us go to your shop now and look at the books.' While the cobbler was rummaging through his accounts, Nasrudin noticed that the Imam also had an outstanding payment.

'I tell you what,' said Nasrudin, 'I will be seeing the Imam later. Why don't I get him to pay you too.' Eagerly, the cobbler agreed.

'He owes three gold pieces.'

'And I owe?'

'Five.'

'And if you take three from five, that makes…'

'Two.'

'Very well, give me the two gold pieces and I will be on my way.'

E

Extraordinary Woman

Nasrudin arrived home from a long journey in the middle of the night. Entering the kitchen he found the stove cold and the cupboards bare. He woke his wife and announced his return.

'It is late. Would you like something to drink before you sleep?' asked his wife, rubbing her eyes.

'What a treasure of a woman you are!' exclaimed Nasrudin. 'Most wives would run about wondering how to find the ingredients for stew at this hour. But you are willing to offer me tea as well.'

E

Extreme Laziness

Nasrudin was summoned by his brother-in-law. 'You have been avoiding me, Nasrudin, ever since I lent you money. Are you not ashamed?' Knowing his in-law to be an exceptionally lazy man, the Mulla replied:

'I have come to repay what I owe. Come over here, shake my hand, remove my purse from my pocket, count out what I owe, replace my purse and bid me farewell.'

'Do you want me to collapse with fatigue?' asked the brother-in-law. 'Go on your way and do not bother me again!'

E

Face your Donkey

Nasrudin was visiting a small town in a foreign land. Finding himself in a teahouse when it was time for the evening prayer, he turned to the proprietor.

'Tell me, which way is the Holy City of Mecca?'

'Wondering which way to pray, are you?' said the man. 'It's obvious that you are new in town. There are so many thieves around here that I suggest you pray facing your donkey.'

F

Fallen off my Donkey

asrudin was riding into town when he passed an orchard. Unable to resist the ripe apples, he manoeuvred his donkey next to the wall, and stretched his arms out to one of the trees. As the fruit was almost in his grasp, a noise startled his donkey and it ran off, leaving Nasrudin dangling from the tree. The orchard owner happened to walk by. Seeing the Mulla struggling in the apple tree, he bellowed:

'Get down, thief, before I get a stick and beat you black and blue!'

'Any fool,' panted Nasrudin, 'can see that I'm not a thief. It is obvious that I have simply fallen off my donkey.'

F

False Evidence

The judge was most displeased when Nasrudin appeared in court to give evidence. He knew the Mulla to be a great believer in the truth, and not the sort of testifier he wanted for this case. Therefore he tried to exclude Nasrudin from the trial.

'Any man testifying in my court must know the Qur'an by heart.'

Nasrudin began to recite verses of the Qur'an in perfect Arabic.

'That's not all: witnesses must also know how to lay out a body for burial.'

'None of the bodies I have laid out have complained.'

Annoyed by this hitch in his plans, the judge tried one last time.

'But do you know the words one should whisper in the ear of the corpse as it is being lowered into the ground?'

'Yes,' replied the Mulla: '"In life, you were indeed fortunate to have been spared the ordeal of giving truthful evidence before our judge."'

F

Family Tradition

Nasrudin was planting a fruit tree in his garden. 'I am glad to see that you are planting an orchard,' said the money-lender. 'The trees will grow and bear fruit which may then be sold to pay off what you owe me.'

'I am planting to follow a family tradition,' replied the Mulla. 'When my great-grandfather realised that his days were numbered, he planted a fruit tree and instructed my grandfather to harvest the fruit after his death. When the crop was finally ready for market, my father, the new generation, picked the fruit and sold it. The money was indeed used to repay debts — those of my great grandfather. Now I am planting similar trees so that my as yet unborn son can tend the trees and instruct his son to pay off what I owe.'

F

Far More Becoming

Nasrudin was so fond of his donkey that he commissioned the tailor to make it a dazzling bridle, decorated with sequins and embroidered flowers. Placing the beautiful head-piece on his beloved ass, he rode off to market to do some shopping. While he was in the bazaar, he tethered the donkey to a post and went into the butcher. Coming out a few minutes later, he was devastated to find the bridle gone. As he made his way home, muttering about the dishonesty all around, he noticed an elegant black mare wearing his donkey's stolen headgear. Going up to the horse, he whispered in its ear:

'I suppose you stole that from my poor donkey because you consider yourself far more beautiful than he, but I can assure you that it was far more becoming on him than it is on you.'

F

Far Too Simple

'Has anyone seen my donkey?' Nasrudin asked a group of youngsters.

'Yes,' said one cheeky lad, 'he has been made chief of police in the next town.'

'Impossible,' replied the Mulla. 'My donkey is not nearly intelligent enough for the job. He is far too simple-minded to frame people and then take their bribes.'

F

Fisherman's Tales

Nasrudin and his friend the baker were fishing when the Mulla reeled in a large trout. He put this in his basket and turned to cast off again. But the other man was so jealous of the Mulla's catch that he removed it from the basket and stuffed it into the pocket of his coat. A few minutes later, he stretched.

'I am too tired to continue; I think I will return home.'

Nasrudin bade him farewell, and tried his luck for a while longer. But soon he too decided to go home. When he had packed up his rod and net, he opened the basket to check on the trout and saw that it had disappeared. Realising that his friend had taken the fish, he wandered home plotting how to get it back.

That evening he was drinking tea with some friends when he saw the baker come into the teahouse.

'Today I caught a trout that was three hands long,' Nasrudin announced.

The baker said nothing. 'Now I come to think about it, it was closer to five hands long,' continued the Mulla.

The baker bit his lip, not daring to challenge Nasrudin's exaggeration. 'When I say five, I really mean ten!' cried the Mulla. 'In fact, it was almost as long as my donkey from ears to tail!'

F

Unable to stand the lies any longer, the baker opened his coat and threw the trout on the table. 'What a braggart you are, Nasrudin! Let everyone witness that the fish is less than two hands long!'

F

Five for the Price of One

Nasrudin returned home from the dentist with a satisfied smile.

'Where have your teeth gone?' demanded his horrified wife, seeing his toothless gums.

'I have just made an excellent deal with the dentist. The extortionist tried to charge me a gold piece for removing a bad tooth, but I haggled and he took out four healthy ones too. Not a bad bargain: five teeth for the price of one.'

F

Five of Us

'Nasrudin,' asked the local Imam, 'how is it that you attend only one out of five daily prayer sessions?'

'Simple mathematics,' replied the Mulla. 'There are five in my family. We are each responsible for one prayer a day.'

F

Following Instructions

Nasrudin desperately needed money to pay his debts. One day, he collected feathers from his chicken coop and fashioned them into fans. As it was summer, there was no shortage of people trying to keep cool. Encouraged by success, Nasrudin tied more feathers together that night and returned to the bazaar the next day. As soon as he set up his stall, he was mobbed by the previous day's customers.

'These are not fans — they are just feathers!' they clamoured. 'As soon as we tried to use them, they fell apart.'

'Unfortunately,' replied Nasrudin, 'I cannot refund your money because you have all failed to follow the instructions.'

'And what might the instructions be?' demanded the angry crowd.

'Take a fan, open it, and move your head from side to side.'

F

Fond Memories

The Mulla's wife was preparing to visit her relatives in India

'I will miss you terribly when I am away,' she moaned.

'And I will naturally miss you,' Nasrudin replied.

'If only I had something of yours to remember you by,' said his wife.

'Such as?'

'If I could take your emerald ring with me, then each time I looked at it I could think of you.'

'You could take it, but if I keep it with me, each time I see it still on my finger I will remember you…'

F

Fool's Gold

Nasrudin was trying to find a chest of gold that he had hidden in the garden. Just as he was digging his first hole, his neighbour came running up and told him that bandits were making the villagers hand over their valuables. On hearing the news, the Mulla dashed all over the garden digging small holes.

'It's no good trying to hide your gold,' snarled the bandit chieftain on entering Nasrudin's garden.

'But that's just it,' replied the Mulla. 'I hid my gold many months ago and now that I'm trying to find it for you, I can't remember where it is buried.'

'Think! Surely you must remember something.'

'Ah yes, it's all coming back to me now,' replied Nasrudin. 'I was standing on the spot where I buried the chest when a bee stung me on the end of the nose.'

F

Forgotten your Face

asrudin's brother-in-law was appointed mayor and the Mulla rushed at once to congratulate him. At the court-house, the new mayor was being measured up for a new cloak. Peering down his nose at the Mulla he said:

'Forgive me but I don't seem to remember your face.'

'I am your brother-in-law.'

'My brother-in-law? What business do you have here?'

'Well,' answered Nasrudin, 'I heard that you had been afflicted by amnesia and came as quickly as I could to offer my help.'

F

For Safe-keeping

One summer's day the mayor was overcome by heat and went to swim in a nearby stream. Nasrudin, who was passing, heard the mayor splashing about and took his turban and coat.

Two days later, the mayor saw Nasrudin in town and recognised his dazzling coat and turban as his own.

'How dare you steal my clothes? I will have you whipped!' he threatened.

'I did not steal your clothes, but took them for safe-keeping. And I am just on my way to your house to return them and collect my reward.'

Four Huntsmen

One day, four huntsmen rode into Nasrudin's village. Knocking on the Mulla's door they asked for water. In accordance with the laws of hospitality, Nasrudin invited them in and asked his wife to bring not only water, but also plates of stew and rice. When the guests had eaten their fill and were preparing to depart, their host pressed a flask into each man's hand.

'Take further refreshment with you and go in peace.'

Three of the horsemen thanked him warmly for the water, but the fourth demanded another flask.

'O Monarch of the World!' bleated the Mulla, 'I had no idea that it was you!'

'That is because I am in disguise,' replied the stunned ruler. 'But how do you now come to recognise me?'

'Your thirst for water is as great as your thirst for power,' replied his host.

F

From Sermons to Sentences

'How is it that you haven't complained about life for at least three days?' Nasrudin's wife asked him.

'Three days ago, I heard that the Imam had applied for the post of judge,' replied her husband.

'Why should that make you happy?'

'I'm not happy,' said Nasrudin. 'I'm just enjoying life until he gets the job. Think how hard life will be when his sermons become sentences.'

F

Friends in High Places

Nasrudin was returning home from market with a cartload of goods. The road was in such poor condition and the sacks on the cart so heavy that the donkey collapsed with fatigue. The Mulla started to curse the animal and then to beat it with a stick.

'I order you to get up! My supper is getting cold at home!'

The Queen, who happened to be looking out of the palace window, called down to the street: 'Stop beating that donkey at once. Can't you see it is exhausted?'

'Excuse me!' Nasrudin whispered, patting the beast, 'I had no idea that you were a close friend of the Queen.'

F

Funeral Guest

When the town judge died, Nasrudin was surprised to be invited to his funeral. 'Don't you remember how he hated me?' he asked the deceased's wife. 'Perhaps it would have been better not to invite me.'

'That is in the past,' replied the widow. 'He is dead now and it is time life moved on.'

'That is what I am afraid of,' muttered Nasrudin. 'Suppose he becomes so reproachful of my presence that he rises from the dead and breaks out of his box. We would never be able to persuade him to return to his coffin.'

F

Goat Defence

When King Tamerlane heard that Nasrudin had been poking fun at some of the country's most eminent religious leaders, he dispatched his guards to arrest the sage.

Luckily, Nasrudin was told that the King's men were on their way, and he had enough time to seek shelter. Leading his prize goat into the mayor's courtyard, he asked for the man's protection.

When his guards came back without the Mulla, Tamerlane himself visited the town and set up a court. Nasrudin was summoned to answer the allegations but, to Tamerlane's surprise, it was the mayor who eloquently put Nasrudin's case.

'Have you yourself nothing to add?' the King asked the defendant.

'No, Your Majesty,' replied the Mulla. 'It sounds as though the goat has told the mayor all he needs to know.'

G

God's Home

Nasrudin's son turned to him one day with a question. 'Father, where does God live?' 'How should I know?' replied the Mulla. 'He has never invited me to visit Him.'

G

Going Hungry

---

*T*he Imam invited Nasrudin to supper, but when the Mulla arrived he found the table bare and the Imam eager to hear his own voice. For several hours, the spiritual leader told tales of prophets and miracles, kings and oppressors, until Nasrudin was practically fainting with hunger.

'Excuse me,' he said eventually.

'You have a question?' asked the Imam, hoping for some religious comment.

'Only one,' replied the Mulla. 'Did any of these people ever eat?'

G

Good Ingredients

The King could not understand why his troops were forever being repulsed by small bands of ferocious men from the Hindu Kush.

'How is it,' he asked a collection of his generals, 'that you lead highly trained fighting men, carrying the most sophisticated weapons and fed on the best rations, into defeat after defeat against these wild foes?'

When none of the leaders could come up with an explanation, Nasrudin, the cook, chipped in:

'It is a matter of ingredients, Your Majesty. The men of the Hindu Kush roam free, they drink the purest water from mountain springs and eat livestock reared on the freshest grass. The strongest ingredients make the strongest men.'

G

Good Intentions

Nasrudin lent his neighbour some money. Unable to repay the debt, the man gave him a cow.

Realising that he had benefited most from the exchange, Nasrudin resolved to give the first bowl of cream to the other man.

Next day, he knocked at his door.

The neighbour was late for market and told Nasrudin to return another time. When the Mulla tried to give him the cream, he became angry.

'Don't you think I have enough trouble selling my own wares without also being asked to sell yours? Clear off, or I'll set the dogs on you!'

That evening, he went to apologise for his earlier short-temper.

'If you would still like me to sell your cream, I'll do so tomorrow.'

'This morning,' said Nasrudin, 'I wanted to give you the cream as a present, but your dogs chased my good intentions out of me. Now my heart is as empty as the bowl.'

G

Grand Judge

'Nasrudin,' said the great Emperor Tamerlane, 'I have decided to appoint you Grand Judge!'

'Indeed an honour, Sire, but I am unworthy.'

'Are you refusing a royal command?'

'I have no choice, Your Majesty. A judge should be a pure and righteous man.'

'True.'

'Well, I have said I am unworthy. If I am telling the truth, then I should not be a judge, and if I am lying, then how can a liar become Grand Judge?'

G

Green Ribbons

Nasrudin took a second wife, but the women were always asking him to choose a favourite. Tiring of their constant vying for the most attention, he went to the bazaar and bought two identical green ribbons. Returning home, he called each wife separately and gave her a ribbon.

'Wear this under your dress, but don't show it off or speak of it to anyone else.'

The next time the two women demanded to know which he preferred he said:

'My favourite is the one wearing a green ribbon beneath her dress.'

G

Grounds for Divorce

'Nasrudin,' said the judge, 'I have asked you to appear in court because your wife has requested a divorce.'

'On what grounds?' asked the Mulla, much surprised by the news.

'She says you have not spoken to her for several days. As you know, dumbness is adequate grounds.'

'And is there not a clause that says that talkativeness is equal grounds? For the only reason that not a word has passed my lips is that she never allows me to get a word in edgeways.'

G

Growing my Field

Someone observed Nasrudin digging earth from his field and piling it into a mound. 'What are you doing, Mulla?' he asked.

'I am collecting this earth so that I can scatter it and make my field grow bigger.'

G

Growing Tall and Strong

*N*asrudin was passing a field when he saw two farmers sowing seed.

'What are you doing?' he asked, never having seen this before.

One of the men, a wag, decided to pull the Mulla's leg.

'We are sowing seed. By morning it will be corn two metres high, and by sunset it will be ready for harvesting.'

'I don't believe you!' grinned the Mulla.

'But surely you know that all things planted in fertile soil grow tall and strong?'

'Then plant me in the ground too!' pleaded Nasrudin. Laughing, the two men dug a hole, placed Nasrudin in it and packed the soil tightly around him. Then they sat down under a nearby tree to eat their lunch. Smelling the spicy pulao, Nasrudin became restless.

'Brothers! I have not sprouted yet. I fear it is because I am too far from the pulao.'

G

Hand-me-downs

On the King's birthday, crowds lined the streets to greet the monarch and his entourage as they paraded through town. Ashamed of his modest dress, Nasrudin sat in an alleyway listening to the festivities.

'O Allah, how can I show myself in public on this important day without so much as a clean shirt?'

At that moment, the cobbler, replacing his torn shirt with a new one bought for the special occasion, changed the garments and threw his old shirt into the street. It landed at Nasrudin's feet. Inspecting the garment — even more ragged than his own — the Mulla snorted:

'Allah! It is most unfair to offer me Your hand-me-downs. I don't want Your charity or Your rags.' And he hurled the shirt back through the open window.

H

Hands Full

During the Tartar conquest of Western Asia, Nasrudin was press-ganged into the army. One day, he found himself part of a division dispatched to suppress rebellion in a border town. Fuelled by resentment, the town's inhabitants easily defeated the Emperor's troops. The few who survived were forced to flee.

When Nasrudin finally returned to the palace, covered in cuts and bruises, Tamerlane attacked him.

'How could you let yourself be beaten? You had your sword and musket.'

'They were my downfall,' replied Nasrudin. 'With weapons in one hand, and my conscience in the other, I had no free hand with which to fight.'

H

Hang On for a Cure

A patient came to see Nasrudin.

'Doctor, all night I am kept awake by a terrible burning in my veins, a throbbing in my head and a ringing in my ears.'

'I suggest you hang on a little longer.'

'And you will have found a cure?'

'No, the illness will run its course and you will rest in eternal peace.'

H

Hard Bargains

asrudin was descending the mountainside, leading his donkey loaded with firewood. The animal lost its footing and fell over the cliff.

'God have mercy! Save this poor beast and I will donate a gold piece to the mosque.' As soon as the words had passed his lips, the donkey landed on a narrow ledge.

'I had no idea that You were so mercenary!' Nasrudin cried to the Heavens. At that moment he saw the ledge starting to crumble under the donkey's weight.

'You misunderstand, God! I am about to offer You a second piece of gold.' But the donkey was unable to clamber up the hill before the ledge crashed into the ravine below.

'I had no idea that You drove such a hard bargain,' said the Mulla, shaking his head sadly, as the donkey disappeared from sight.

H

Hazardous Food

asrudin had been invited to a banquet, but when he arrived, dressed in his most presentable clothes, he was seated with the servants. The host, an old adversary, wanted to humiliate Nasrudin in public. Seeing that there was also a free place to the right of the guest of honour, Nasrudin went and sat himself down there.

When the food was served, he was surprised to see that the guests were served plain rice, while the host and his guest of honour were presented with platters of steaming pulao. Without a word, Nasrudin reached over and loaded his plate with meat and gravy from his host's dish.

'Careful, Mulla,' advised the man in his ear, 'you may find the food extremely hazardous to your health.'

Turning to the man, Nasrudin smiled sweetly, 'I feared as much, my Lord, and thought that my stomach should be sacrificed so that you might be spared the pain of the hazardous food.'

H

Heaven and Hell

amerlane, the Ruler of the World, summoned Nasrudin in order to discuss philosophical matters.

'Tell me, sage,' he asked, 'which is larger, Heaven or Hell?'

'That depends on who goes to Heaven and who to Hell,' Nasrudin answered.

'We already know,' said the Emperor. 'The righteous go to Heaven and the sinners go to Hell.'

'If all bandits, tyrants, and oppressors go down and all virtuous men go up,' said Nasrudin, 'then Heaven must be the larger place.'

'And how do you reach that conclusion?' asked Tamerlane.

'Conquerors such as yourself are in short supply,' replied Nasrudin, 'but each ruler has many subjects.'

H

Heaven is Full

'Nasrudin,' said the judge, 'you claim to know of the Other World — so tell me, is Heaven overcrowded?'

'Your Honour,' replied the sage, 'it is splitting at the seams.'

'How is that?'

'Thanks to magistrates such as yourself, the angels have barely enough time to receive newcomers before another man leaves the gallows.'

Heavenly Flock

*T*he inhabitants of Nasrudin's village were so miserly that, while he was Imam, there were seldom enough donations for him to live on. One day, he resolved to put the matter right.

'Look at our humble place of worship,' he added in his sermon. 'In Heaven there used to be a mosque so beautiful that it shimmered from dawn to dusk. But due to the meanness of the heavenly congregation, the Imam starved to death and it had to close.'

Heaven or Hell?

A group of traders were discussing the death of the town's mayor

'Never have we had such a corrupt and greedy man,' said one. 'If he has gone to Paradise, I will divorce my young and beautiful wife and leave the town.'

'God works in mysterious ways,' said another. 'The mayor may well have had his slate wiped clean and been welcomed in Paradise.'

'Nasrudin,' said a third, 'you claim to have all the answers. Has the mayor gone to Heaven or Hell?'

After a few moments consideration the Mulla replied: 'No man can say how the Almighty makes such decisions. The mayor may be sitting in Paradise as we speak.'

The traders agreed, and looked expectantly at the merchant who had vowed to leave town.

'But,' continued Nasrudin, 'if Allah is magnanimous enough to forgive the mayor for the atrocities he committed while alive, He would certainly pardon a few hasty promises made by our friend here and permit him to stay with his new bride.'

H

Hereditary

---

*N*asrudin was unemployed and decided to set himself up as a doctor. One day, an elderly neighbour came to him and asked his professional advice:

'My brother and his wife have been trying to have children for many years, but with no success. What could be the cause of their problem?'

'There are several possible causes,' replied Nasrudin. 'For example, it could be hereditary. Was your brother's mother unable to have children?'

H

He Will be Here Soon

*N*asrudin was minding his fruit stall when a thief made off with a sack of apples. The Mulla asked a friend to mind his wares and then he set off for the cemetery.

'What are you doing sitting in the graveyard?' asked his neighbour, walking by several hours later.

'I am waiting for the thief who took my apples. His sort inevitably end up here.'

H

Hidden Strength

*N*asrudin tasted alcohol for the first time, and then went to find his donkey. Approaching the animal, he took up the reins and led the donkey behind him.

'How strange that people say a man has but to look at a drink and he becomes intoxicated,' he chuckled, not feeling in the least bit drunk. 'I must have a metabolism far superior to others.'

'What do you think?' he asked his donkey over his shoulder. 'Shall I go and have another glass?'

'I wouldn't, father,' replied his young son, on the other end of the lead.

H

Hiding

One day, Nasrudin's wife went into the kitchen and lit the stove. She then went to get some water from the well. Re-entering the house, she thought she heard her husband calling to her, but he was nowhere to be seen. Going back into the kitchen, she realised that screams were coming from the oven. She opened the oven door and Nasrudin rolled out.

'What on earth are you doing in the oven?' asked the surprised woman.

'I was hiding from the call to prayer,' grumbled the Mulla, patting the flames from his coat. 'But now you've opened the oven door I can hear the voice of the muezzin and I am obliged to go to the mosque.'

High and Low

asrudin's friend inherited some money and moved into a mansion in the centre of town.

'You never greet me in the street these days,' Nasrudin said to his friend when the two happened to meet. 'Can it be that you have forgotten your old friends?'

'Quite the reverse,' lied his friend, 'I have become so used to walking around my cast iron balcony and looking down in the hope of seeing someone I know, that it has become a habit to hang my head. I therefore never recognise acquaintances when I meet them in the street.'

A few days later, the Mulla walked straight past the same friend with his eyes to the sky.

'Have you become so lofty that you no longer greet a friend in the street?' asked the friend.

'Quite the reverse,' replied Nasrudin, 'I have simply become so used to my friends rising above me that I have taken to walking along looking up, in the hope that I might catch a glimpse of them strolling on their balconies.'

H

His own Ban

*D*uring the Tartar conquest of Western Asia, Tamerlane sent his troops into battle time after time. As a result of these costly campaigns, taxation soared. The poor were forced to hand over the last of their meagre possessions, while praying for peace.

When the despot's spies told him of the discontent sweeping the Empire, he sent his criers to announce that any man, woman or child uttering the word 'peace' would be executed.

Not long after this decree, Nasrudin returned to the Court after many months absence. Tamerlane was delighted to see the sage again and greeted him warmly: 'Peace be upon you!'

Instead of returning the greeting, Nasrudin began to call for the executioner, who duly appeared, sword in hand. 'In accordance with the absolute monarch's wishes, you must now cut off his head!' Nasrudin told the astonished man. 'He has broken his own ban on pronouncing the word "peace". Now let him receive his own punishment.'

H

Hit the Wrong Man

One day, Nasrudin was shopping in the bazaar when a man walked up behind him and slapped him on the back of the head.

'I must apologize,' said his attacker as the Mulla spun round. 'I thought you were someone else.'

Not satisfied with an apology, Nasrudin took the man to court. But it turned out that he was the nephew of the judge, who was reluctant to start proceedings.

When an hour had passed and the magistrate still refused to start the hearing, Nasrudin walked up to him and boxed him on the ear.

'Oh, forgive me, Your Honour, but this stranger hit me and I think the blow was originally meant for you.'

H

Hole after Hole

Nasrudin's neighbour looked over the fence and saw the Mulla digging a large hole.
'Replanting?'

'No, I am going to bury the rubble left from building the house. It is taking up half of the garden.'

'What will you do with the earth?'

'I'll dig another hole for that.'

Holy Donkey

'Mulla,' said one of his disciples, 'your donkey is more of a true believer than you.'
'How so?' asked Nasrudin.

'Well,' the young man continued, 'offer your beast the choice between a bucket of water and a bucket of wine and he will surely opt for the water.'

'All that proves,' replied the Mulla, 'is that my donkey is less intelligent than I.'

H

Hospitality

Although poor, Nasrudin set great store by hospitality. One evening, the local Imam paid a surprise visit. Determined to receive such an important man in style, Nasrudin killed his last goat and served it to the guest. He then sat and watched as the notable — a man of considerable appetite — devoured the entire roast together with every other morsel of food in the house.

So good was the meal that the Imam resolved to pay another visit as soon as possible. He arrived the next evening and sat at the table singing the praises of his host:

'May Allah deliver blessings to this most generous man and permit him to serve his honoured guest with a meal as flavoursome as yesterday's goat.'

Nasrudin disappeared into the kitchen and came back with the bare goat's carcass. The Imam was most surprised.

'Is this some sort of joke? Where is the food?'

'As your host I must do as you say. You just asked me to bring yesterday's goat and here it is. How can I help it if this is all that remains?'

H

House Calls

Nasrudin was collecting firewood in the mountains. He was cursing himself for travelling so far from home without having thought to pack anything to eat, when a stranger appeared and cried:

'My brother is very ill. Where can I find a doctor?'

'I am a doctor,' replied Nasrudin, and he was immediately led to the patient's house. On entering, he was given a large bowl of pulao and a pot of green tea. When he had finished his meal, he turned his attentions to the sick man.

'Cover him with more blankets and place his feet in iced water,' he told the patient's wife before leaving the house.

He had hardly gone a few yards when the man caught up with him.

'So much for your medical advice! My brother has just expired!'

'That is unfortunate,' replied Nasrudin, 'but look on the bright side. If I had not had that pulao, I might have died too!'

H

How Did they all Know?

One day, Nasrudin turned to his pupils and said: 'If anyone can tell me what I have in my pocket, I will give them a blue marble with green swirls.'

The entire class started to laugh and yell: 'Blue and green marbles! Blue and green marbles!'

'I am not sure I will have enough to go round,' said Nasrudin, wondering how on earth they had all guessed correctly.

H

How Long will I Live?

One night Tamerlane dreamt that he was on his death-bed and was destined for the burning fires of Hell. Much troubled by the nightmare, he called his astrologers.

'How long shall I live?' he asked each man in turn.

The first told the Emir he would live for twenty years. The second, that he would live fifty years. The third that he would live a hundred years. And the fourth told the Emir that he would never die.

'Executioner!' roared Tamerlane, 'behead these men. Three have given me too little time and the fourth is just trying to save his own neck.' Then, turning to Nasrudin he said:

'You have told my fortune on occasion. What have you to say?'

The Mulla calmly replied: 'Great Emperor, it just so happens that I, too, had a dream last night in which an angel told me the exact day of your demise.'

'And what did he say?' Tamerlane anxiously asked.

'The angel told me that you would die on the very same day as I,' replied Nasrudin.

H

How to be Wise

'Father,' asked Nasrudin's youngest son one day, 'how can I become as wise as you?'

'If a knowledgeable man is talking, listen to him,' replied the Mulla, 'and if you are talking, listen to yourself.'

How to Fall Asleep

'Not asleep yet, Mulla?' asked his house guest.

'What of it?'

'I was wondering if you could lend me some money.'

'Can't you see I am deeply asleep!' exclaimed Nasrudin, throwing the blankets over his face.

How to Find a Bride

Nasrudin's oldest son was looking for a wife. 'Which qualities are you seeking?' Nasrudin asked the youth.

'Intelligence rather than beauty,' replied the young man.

'If that is the case,' said the Mulla, 'I have an excellent way of finding you the perfect bride.' He told the youth to follow and went into town. When they reached the main square, Nasrudin started to cuff his son and shout:

'How dare you do exactly as I say? This is the punishment fit for one who obeys!'

'Leave him alone!' hissed one young woman, 'How can you beat him for being a model son?'

'This is surely the woman for me, father,' said Nasrudin's son.

'Best to have a choice,' replied the Mulla and led the way to the neighbouring town. Here, he acted out exactly the same scene. But this time, a young girl began to cheer him on:

'That's right! Hit him! Only a fool obeys blindly.'

'Son,' said Nasrudin, with a smile, 'I think we have found you an intelligent bride.'

H

Human Nature

*N*asrudin was once the student of a sage renowned for his understanding of human nature. One day, one of the wise man's disciples brought a plate of confectionery to his master as an offering. Noting Nasrudin's keen interest in the sweets, the wise man warned him to avoid the plate as the food was laced with a deadly poison. He then left the room. Nasrudin, enticed by the aroma of honey and almonds, picked up the plate and inadvertently dropped it and the delicacies on the floor. He quickly swept up the broken china and frenziedly ate up the sweets. The sage returned and started to shout:

'Who dared to move my plate?'

'Alas!' sighed the distraught Nasrudin, clutching his stomach, 'I broke your valuable plate but I chose death as my punishment, and ate up all the poison!'

H

I Cannot be Rebuilt

Nasrudin was riding through the countryside when the forest burst into flames. As villages were being consumed by the fire to the left and right of the path, Nasrudin rode calmly on, repeating: 'Thanks to Allah! Thanks to Allah!'

'How can you thank Allah when all around you our possessions, houses and fields are being burnt to a crisp?' wailed an old woman fleeing the flames.

'Possessions can be replaced. Houses can be rebuilt and fields can be replanted. I am thanking Allah for keeping my donkey calm. If he panicked, he could throw me from his back and trample me underfoot and, unlike a house, I cannot be rebuilt.'

Identified by a Goat

One morning, Nasrudin found that someone else's goat had wandered into his paddock. Seizing the animal, he immediately killed it and gave it to his wife to cook. Later, he felt ashamed of the theft and confided in a friend.

'How could you steal another's goat? Are you not afraid of suffering the wrath of God?' asked the man.

'I will tell Allah I know nothing of the incident,' replied the Mulla.

'But Allah might call the goat to identify you.'

'In that case, I'll be able to grab the goat and return it to its rightful owner.'

If it Pleases Allah

*I*t is customary for Muslims to say: 'If it pleases Allah' before undertaking any affair, be it big or small.

One day, Nasrudin said to his wife:

'If it is good weather tomorrow, I shall go to the market and buy a new donkey.'

'You have forgotten to add: "If it pleases Allah",' replied his wife.

But Nasrudin, exasperated by a string of misfortunes, was sulking. 'It never does seem to please Allah, and I am sick of saying the words when they do no good,' he said sullenly.

Next day was sunny and the Mulla set off for the donkey auction, where he bought an ass for a very reasonable price. Sitting on his new donkey, he started for home.

'Who needs the good wishes of God?' he said happily to himself. 'I have found a true bargain without His approval.'

Just then a snake slithered across the path. The terrified donkey bucked and Nasrudin flew into the air and landed in a thorn bush. As he struggled to free himself, the roots of the bush came away and the Mulla was thrown downhill.

After much rolling and bumping, the bush landed at the base of the slope and Nasrudin managed to extricate himself from the thorns. Bruised and bleeding, with his clothes ripped to shreds, he limped the rest of the way home.

He was so far from his village that he did not reach his house until night had fallen and his wife had locked the door.

With the last of his strength he knocked.

'Who is there?' said his wife from inside.

'Open up, wife,' Nasrudin replied faintly, 'It is I, if it pleases Allah.'

If I were You

One winter Nasrudin rode high into the mountains in search of firewood. After a day of exhausting work, he finally had enough branches piled on his donkey to return home. But soon, he could stand the biting cold no longer. Thanking God for the fact that he at least had wood for a fire, he set light to the bundles on the donkey's back. With a bray of alarm, the beast galloped off at full speed.

'If I were you,' Nasrudin hollered after the animal, 'I'd jump in the nearest river!'

I

If Only I had Known Earlier

The Imam was going through a spiritual crisis. 'Satan has tempted me and I have become confused in my belief,' he moaned, tearing at his beard. 'Nasrudin, you are a sage with an understanding of religion. What shall I do?'

'If only you had asked my advice earlier,' replied the Mulla. 'A while back, the Devil approached me with similar complaints about you. He said you had caused him to re-evaluate his position. If I had known you felt the same, I would have put him directly in touch with you.'

If You are What You Say

Nasrudin was sitting discussing matters of a philosophical nature with other learned men. But their conversation was constantly interrupted with thoughtless remarks made by a man outside the circle.

'Are you a complete good-for-nothing?' snapped the Mulla, tiring of the man's interruptions.

'How dare you suggest I am a nothing?' replied the other. 'I am a cobbler!'

Hearing this, Nasrudin removed his slippers and ripped them apart. Handing them to the cobbler he said:

'If you are what you say, you will be able to mend these. Bring them back as good as new in an hour's time and I will believe you.' Without waiting to be asked again, the man hurried off to mend the slippers.

If Your Tongue was Mine

One evening the town poet was reciting his latest work. One by one, the audience tired of the verse and slipped away. Soon only Nasrudin was left alone with the bard.

'At least there is one person who appreciates my work,' said the artist. 'Tell me, Mulla, are there any comments you would like to make?'

Nasrudin remained silent.

'Have my glorious words caused you to lose your tongue?'

'If your tongue was mine,' replied the Mulla, 'I would have torn it out long ago.'

Immodest

Nasrudin had long intended to ask for the hand of a certain young girl. But before he had saved the money for her dowry, his friend told him that he was to wed the beauty. The Mulla was very upset and, thinking for a moment, he said:

'I congratulate you, she is indeed a prize. In fact, I was talking to another man only today, who admitted he was quite dazzled by her loveliness.'

'Are you saying that she has appeared unveiled in public?' asked his friend.

'I am simply repeating what I have heard,' replied Nasrudin.

Much shaken, the other man hurried to his prospective father-in-law's house and broke off the engagement.

A few months later, when Nasrudin had finally secured the money for the dowry, he became engaged to the girl. When his friend heard the news, he was very annoyed.

'If you had not implied that the girl was immodest, I would have married her myself!'

'You are confused,' said Nasrudin calmly, 'I never so much as hinted that she was immodest.'

'But you said you had spoken to another man who was dazzled by her beauty.'

'Didn't I mention that the other man was her father?' asked Nasrudin.

Impossible

'Nasrudin,' said his neighbour, 'have you heard, the judge has lost his mind?'

'Impossible,' replied the Mulla. 'How can he have lost something he never had?'

Impromptu Speeches

*P*assing the town hall, Nasrudin saw an interesting scrap of paper pinned to the top of the notice board. Try as he might he couldn't make out the words, so he got up on to an old box in order to have a closer look. Soon a crowd gathered in expectation: 'The Mulla is going to make a speech.'

Turning to face the throng, Nasrudin felt obliged to say a few words.

'Friends!' he cried, 'As you know, I am not usually short of a speech or two, but I must admit that this time you have caught me unawares and I don't have an idea in my head.'

His wife spoke from somewhere in the centre of the crush. 'Not even the idea of getting down and coming home to supper?'

In Advance

For several years, Nasrudin worked for a banker. When the time came for him to leave the man's employ, he went to collect his wages but was told that he would have to wait until the necessary funds were available.

'But I have worked for ten years without ever having received a single penny,' the Mulla complained.

'Then take this penny as an advance and I will call you when I have the rest,' replied the man, and showed Nasrudin the door.

Without the money he was owed, Nasrudin was unable to journey to Samarkand as he had planned and instead took a job as a grave-digger. One day, he dug a large pit in the cemetery.

'Who is that for?' asked a passer-by.

'The banker.'

'But he is not dead. I saw him only a few minutes ago.'

'The next time you see him, tell him I have prepared his grave in advance.'

In a Ravenous Hurry

Nasrudin was in a strange city when he heard music and laughter coming from a colossal mansion. Assuming that a banquet was being held, he went up to the gate, trying to think of a way he could gain entrance to the festivities.

'I have an important message from the King,' he told the guards, and was instantly ushered into the house. The host, delighted to be seen receiving the King's envoy, called for the choicest dishes to be laid on the table before Nasrudin.

When the King's servant had eaten his fill, the host asked him what news he brought from the palace.

'I was in such a hurry to reach you before the pulao ran out, that I left before the King gave me the message,' replied Nasrudin.

In Charge of the List

Nasrudin was not a popular Imam and was continually being demoted, until he found himself in a remote hamlet full of farmers not known for their generosity. Most of their donations to the mosque consisted of carrots and apples, a diet against which their spiritual leader soon rebelled.

One day, in an address after the morning prayers, Nasrudin made an important announcement:

'I have been asked to inform you that from now on it has fallen upon me to draw up a list of those of you destined for Heaven and those of you destined for Hell.'

From that day on, the Imam was never short of fresh meat, butter, cream and pulao.

Incomplete Chickens

Nasrudin was taking a present of a roast chicken to his father-in-law. It was a long trip, and he soon became ravenously hungry. Unable to resist the delicious meat, he removed one of the wings and ate it. But the small amount did not even begin to satisfy his rumbling stomach and so, a few miles down the road, he ate a chicken leg. When he arrived at his in-laws, his host was offended by the mangled offering.

'After all these years, you still do not show me the respect I deserve!' he complained.

'But all the chickens in the land were hatched incomplete this year,' replied Nasrudin.

His father-in-law immediately had his cook shoot two of his chickens and bring them to him. 'Look,' he said, dangling the birds in front of his son-in-law, 'these birds are whole!'

'If a cook was pointing a gun at you,' said Nasrudin, 'would you not use your whole body to escape?'

1

Inconsiderate

*N*asrudin had been invited to a wedding. Immaculately dressed, he went to collect his donkey from the pasture behind his house. Seeing the animal rolling on his back, he rushed up and grabbed it by the neck.

'You are so inconsiderate! Not for a moment have you stopped to look at my unblemished apparel and thought that I might want you to make an effort with your appearance too! Instead you roll around in the mud.'

The donkey, resentful of the Mulla's firm grip on his neck, brayed loudly.

'Apologise all you like,' said Nasrudin through gritted teeth, 'but the damage is already done!'

Indecision

One day, the Shah was praising the head cook for the appetising pulao he had prepared. 'There is nothing more fit for a king than pulao!'

'Indeed,' agreed Nasrudin, who was a guest at the royal table.

The King continued to eat greedily. After his fourth serving he started to feel a heaviness in his stomach. 'Actually, pulao is rather filling. There is too much oil — this food is far too rich.'

'Indeed,' agreed the Mulla.

The monarch turned testily to Nasrudin. 'When I praised the food you agreed, and now I fault it you also agree. Are you incapable of forming your own opinion?'

'My Sovereign,' replied the Mulla, 'if a great ruler such as yourself is unable to make up his mind, how can a lesser man such as I ever hope to do so?'

Infernal Snoring

Nasrudin's friend invited him to go on holiday with some other men from the village. Each day, they hunted, wrestled, gambled and generally celebrated the absence of their wives. But on the third day, Nasrudin started to notice the cold stares he was getting from the other holiday makers.

'Why do you look at me with such dislike?' he finally asked.

'Because we are kept awake each night by your infernal snoring.'

When the Mulla heard this, he immediately started to pack his things.

'There is no need to return home, Nasrudin,' said his friend.

'Yes there is,' replied the Mulla. 'I have been married for fifteen years and have slept beside my wife for all that time. Not once has the unfortunate woman complained.'

Inherited Talent

Nasrudin detested the town poet's verses so much that he excused himself from any social gathering at which the man was present. One day he came face to face with the bard, and had no choice but to greet him.

'And who is this?' the Mulla asked, turning to the toddler at the poet's side.

'This is my son. I am teaching him my art. One day, I hope that he will be as fine a poet as his father.'

'Not even in my worst nightmares,' said Nasrudin, 'had I considered a second generation.'

In my Own Time

The Angel of Death came to Nasrudin one day and announced:

'Your time has come, Mulla! Prepare to be taken to the other world.' Trembling and shaking with fear, his face as white as a sheet, Nasrudin managed to choke out a few words:

'My life has been spent blaspheming, and generally poking fun at religion at every possible opportunity. But I am a Muslim, and wish that I could have one last chance to prove that all my past misdemeanours are deeply regretted.'

'What chance do you want?' asked the angel.

'If I could be spared the time to perform the five prayers before my death,' sighed Nasrudin, 'I am sure I would go peacefully on my way.'

'Very well,' replied the angel, 'I will return this time tomorrow when you have performed your five prayers.' And he disappeared. Next day he arrived at the appointed time.

'You have had your extra day of life, Nasrudin. Now you must come with me.'

'Did you not promise to allow me to perform my five prayers before my death?'

'That is so.'

'Well I have performed only two.'

'And when will you say the rest?'

'In my own time.'

In Need of Correction

Nasrudin moved into a new house and, according to legal requirements of the time, went to have the ownership papers signed by the judge. Knowing the magistrate to be a greedy man accustomed to taking bribes, he took with him a tray of sweets.

As soon as the judge saw the dazzling array of confectionery, he signed and stamped the necessary papers. Later, after the evening meal, he signalled for the sweets to be brought, and popped several into his mouth. The whole assortment turned out to be made of wax.

Next day, Nasrudin was sitting with some friends in the bazaar when a servant of the court arrived.

'The judge says there is a problem with yesterday's paperwork and orders you to come back so that any errors can be corrected.'

'It is not a problem with the documentation, but a problem with the judge,' replied Nasrudin. 'Tell him that it is his conscience that is in need of correction, and only God can see to that.'

Inside Out or Outside In?

The King's guards were building a high wall round the treasury.

'Why are you doing this?' asked Nasrudin.

'To stop thieves from getting over,' replied one of the men.

'Those from inside or outside?' asked the Mulla.

Interest

'Nasrudin,' said an impoverished neighbour, 'could you lend me some money? I'll pay whatever rate of interest you demand.'

'My friend,' replied the Mulla, 'I would never take advantage of your misfortune by charging you interest. But unfortunately I have no money to lend.'

I Should Know

*L*ate one night, a burglar broke into Nasrudin's house. Under the cover of darkness, he began to pick up the Mulla's possessions and stuff them into a sack.

'Brother,' said the Mulla, 'I am compelled to warn you that the things you are taking may seem valuable at night but will prove worthless by daylight. I should know.'

Itchy Palms

Nasrudin was once appointed chief of police, but was voted out of office almost immediately. Some days after his dismissal, his wife noticed that he had begun to scratch his right palm.

'I have never noticed that habit before, Nasrudin.'

'That is because my right hand only started to itch when I became chief of police,' replied her husband.

Jaliz, the Eagle

One day, Nasrudin was invited to join a gathering of religious leaders. The revered men took great delight in showing off their own knowledge of Islam. One speculated about the colour of the Prophet's horse, another about the favourite food of the angels. A third gave an extremely long-winded account of the creation of the world, and a fourth a detailed description of Heaven. Finally, Nasrudin could stand the men's conceit no longer.

'Jaliz!' he boomed, much to the amazement of the spiritual leaders.

'Is that a name, Mulla?' asked one.

'Of course!' exclaimed the Mulla, 'I am surprised you need to ask. That was the name of the eagle that swooped down and carried off Moses.'

'But there is no record of Moses being carried off by a bird,' clamoured the gathering.

'Then Jaliz is the name of the eagle that swooped down and didn't carry off Moses,' said Nasrudin with a haughty look.

J

Just a Humble Loaf

*H*earing that all the healthy men in the village were being rounded up and pressed into the army, Nasrudin ran into the kitchen and hid in the oven.

'Tell them I have gone to India,' he told his wife. Refusing to take any excuses, the sergeant's men searched the house and found the Mulla in the oven.

'As an adult male, you are hereby enlisted into His Majesty's forces,' said the officer.

'But I am just a humble loaf,' answered Nasrudin.

'Nonsense!' bellowed the sergeant. 'Come out of there at once!'

'Very well,' replied the Mulla, 'but not until I am fully cooked.'

J

Just Ask

Nasrudin was caught climbing into his neighbour's chicken house.

'I am surprised at you, Mulla, a man of your age, creeping into my coop like a young thief in the night. Were you to come to me as a neighbour and ask for a bird, you could have it.'

'You are quite right. A man of my advanced years could slip and twist an ankle, or cut his fingers on the fence. Therefore, I would be delighted to accept your neighbourly offer of a chicken.'

J

Just in Case

scaping from a band of ferocious brigands, Nasrudin sought refuge in the nearby mountains. Here he met an emaciated man dressed in a ragged coat.

'There is no time to waste,' cried the Mulla. 'You must hide — cut-throats and murderers are right behind me.'

'I am a dervish,' replied the man. 'All my time is spent in reflection and prayer. Allah will not allow anything to happen to his servant.'

'Quite so,' agreed Nasrudin, 'but if I were you I would take the added precaution of hiding, just in case.'

Just Keeping him Company

One day, Nasrudin lost all his money at dice. Returning home, he said to his wife:

'I met a neighbour in the square who had just lost all his money gambling.'

'Thank God that you are not such a foolish man!' barked his wife.

'But I am a good neighbour,' replied Nasrudin, 'and so I had to keep the poor fellow company.'

J

Just Like his Mother

Nasrudin was hurrying to the bazaar one afternoon when an elderly man stopped him and asked:

'Am I mistaken, or are you the son of Jamal, the miller?'

'You are not mistaken,' the Mulla replied hastily. 'I am Jamal's son. Unfortunately, I am a little busy at the moment.'

'My little chap!' wept the man, embracing Nasrudin, 'I have not seen you since you were a baby. You were the sweetest child. I used to play with you for hours on end and tell you stories until you fell asleep on my lap. How long ago was that? It must have been at least forty years. But I would have recognised you anywhere. Your eyes, your hair, your chin... it's true what they say: some men grow to be the spitting images of their fathers.'

'And some grow to twitter on like their mothers!' interrupted the Mulla crossly.

J

Just Reward

*N*asrudin had caused the Imam to lose face so many times that the man eventually hired a group of heavies to beat some respect into his adversary. One night, the ruffians cornered Nasrudin in a dark alley and were about to carry out their orders when the Mulla slipped past them and escaped. Running into town he saw the Imam.

'Why so out of breath, Nasrudin? You flee as if a pack of hungry lions was in hot pursuit.'

'I wish it were only lions,' panted the Mulla, 'but actually the whole village is chasing me because they want to elect me mayor.'

The Imam had been dreaming of becoming mayor for quite some time. 'If I were in your shoes, I would take the job at once.'

'Take all my clothes and the post will be yours,' said Nasrudin, exchanging his clothes with the other man. 'My supporters will be along any second; say nothing when they approach you and by the time they discover their mistake it will be too late.'

The Imam concealed his face in Nasrudin's cloak and waited silently for the mob. Mistaking him for their target, the group of ruffians gave him a good thrashing.

J

Just Testing

The Imam was talking to a gathering in the village square.

'Only the most awe-inspiring figures in history — the great prophets — were able to perform miracles,' he exclaimed.

'Could they raise the dead?' asked Nasrudin.

'Of course,' replied the Imam, 'the Qur'an describes many such events.'

'Then,' said the Mulla, 'I am willing to prove that any man can perform miracles similar to the prophets.'

'Are you daring to suggest that you too can raise the dead?' gasped the Imam.

'Bring me a sword and I will demonstrate,' replied Nasrudin. A sword was brought and the crowd craned their necks to see the miracle.

'What are you going to do?' asked the Imam as Nasrudin pointed the blade toward him.

'I am going to cut your head off so that we can all have a few moments peace, and then I shall replace your head and you will feel as good as new.'

'No need for a demonstration,' the Imam replied nervously. 'I just wanted to test you. Naturally, I know full well that you are able to perform miracles.'

Just the Judge

he judge, a conceited and foolish man, was worried by the lack of respect the inhabitants of the town had shown him. He commissioned the carpenter to build a high platform, from which he could hear evidence and pass sentence. When the structure was finished, he invited Nasrudin — one of the least respectful inhabitants of the town — to come and have a look.

'Almighty Allah,' intoned the Mulla, throwing himself down at the base of the rostrum, 'your humble servant has arrived!'

'Are you mad?' spluttered the judge, 'I am not God.'

'Forgive me, Great Prophet!' wept Nasrudin.

'I am not a prophet either,' screamed the judge.

'Then you must surely be an angel,' replied Nasrudin.

Losing patience, the judge summoned his guards. 'Take this man away and lock him up until he has recovered his senses!'

'Ah,' said Nasrudin, 'with your throne so high, I could not make you out at first. But on the strength of your behaviour, I guess that you are just the town judge.'

J

Keeping an Eye Out

Nasrudin was taking his last sheep to the market to sell. On the way, a friend asked the Mulla to join him for some tea. Accepting the offer at once, the Mulla sat the sheep down at the table and took his place directly opposite.

'My friend,' said his astounded host, 'I asked you to be my guest for tea; I never said you could invite a sheep. Is this meant to be some sort of insult?'

'Certainly not,' replied Nasrudin. 'This simply means that a man with one sheep left in the world should keep an eye on his livestock.'

Keeping Sleep Away

Nasrudin was once the watchman for a cruel and unpopular judge. His employer, an insomniac, had a habit of roaming his grounds in the middle of the night fretting about his enemies. On one such occasion, he found Nasrudin under a blanket snoring loudly.

'Wake up this instant! Your snores could cost me my life.'

'But I'm not asleep,' replied Nasrudin, 'I'm snoring to stop myself dozing off.'

K

Knowing the Name

Nasrudin was so sick of his wife's constant nagging that he decided to divorce her. 'What is your wife's name?' asked the judge. 'I have no idea,' replied Nasrudin.

'You have been married for twenty years and you don't know her name?'

'Why should I know the name of a woman I mean to divorce?' replied Nasrudin.

K

Large Sparrows

Nasrudin returned from his travels with an ostrich egg which he gave to his son to tend. Soon the egg hatched, and the boy raised the bird until it had grown to an enormous size. One day, when father and son were feeding the pet, the judge strode by. Never having seen such a bird, he asked:

'What is this amazing creature?'

'It was once a humble sparrow,' replied Nasrudin, 'but, thanks to bountiful Allah, it has continued to triple in size each day.'

'Is there any hope that I, too, might raise such a prize?'

'No reason why not,' replied Nasrudin, 'if you offer alms to the poor and prayers to God.'

The judge hurried off to the bazaar where he bought three dozen sparrows and distributed two purses of gold to the poor. Back home, he placed the sparrows in a huge cage and instructed his servants to feed them with the best food money could buy. He then locked himself in his room and began to pray.

After several days of supplication, the judge staggered out to inspect his flock. The birds were still the same size. He went to see Nasrudin.

'You are a fraud. The sparrows have not grown.'

L

'Forgive me, Your Honour,' said the Mulla, 'but did you distribute alms to the poor?'

'Yes.'

'And have you beseeched Allah for assistance?'

'Yes, I have spent the last two weeks at prayer.'

Nasrudin thought for a moment:

'I don't suppose you have restricted the birds' movements?'

'I have them in a cage.'

'That is where you are going wrong. The confinement has limited their room for growth.'

When the judge got home, he threw open the cage door and the sparrows — delighted to be free — flew away.

L

Last In, First Out

'*I* am an artist of considerable talent,' boasted the town poet, a foolish and pompous man. 'My works lift the spirits of even the most illiterate peasant. I never cease to marvel at my brilliance and triumphs.'

'Actually,' said Nasrudin, 'I regularly manage to outdo all the people of this town, including yourself.'

The bard stroked his immaculate beard and laughed. 'How can you say that?'

'Whenever you perform one of your rhymes in public, I stand at the back of the room, close to the door. I am the last man to arrive and the first to make my escape.'

L

Laughter and Tears

Nasrudin hated the smell of onions, but his wife liked them so much that she could eat them until tears streamed from her eyes. Every time she included onions in her cooking, she and Nasrudin fought. Finally, their arguments became so fierce that their neighbours took them to court for disturbing the peace. Hearing both sides, the judge told the woman to sign a statement to the effect that she would stop serving onions or her husband would be entitled to an instant divorce.

Several weeks passed, and meal after meal was served without onions. But, with her husband out of the house all day, the woman gradually started to succumb to her craving for onions.

One day, she was tucking into a large plate of the raw vegetable when Nasrudin arrived home unexpectedly. She hardly had enough time to hide the plate before he came into the kitchen. Smelling the pungent aroma of onions, and seeing his wife's streaming eyes, he knew exactly what she had been eating, but was amused by her guilt.

'Why are you crying, my dear?' he asked, adopting a sympathetic tone.

'I am crying for joy because you are home,' replied the woman.

Nasrudin was so pleased by the game that he burst out laughing.

L

'Why are you laughing?' his wife asked in surprise.

'I am laughing because I will soon be free,' replied Nasrudin, 'but in a moment I will be crying too, because I have a terrible feeling that I have lost the statement you signed in court.'

L

Left-handed Hooves

*N*asrudin received an invitation to join a nobleman for a day's hunting. Unaccustomed to such grand events, the Mulla was worried that his lack of riding experience would show. With this in mind, he bribed the nobleman's equerry to lend him the hunter he was to ride on the big day. In secret, he practised mounting and dismounting until he had mastered the manoeuvre.

On the day of the hunt the Mulla swaggered to the stables full of confidence, but was dismayed to find that the horse he had trained on had gone lame, and an unfamiliar animal had been saddled up in its place. Nervously, the Mulla got onto the horse's back. Relieved to find that he had executed the mount without apparent hitch, he prepared to ride off. Reaching for the reins, he realised that he was facing the animal's tail.

'Why was I not informed that this was a left-handed horse?' he angrily asked the stable hand.

L

Left or Right?

'Mulla,' said his elderly neighbour, 'I am told you know a great many useful facts. So tell me, during a funeral, should one stand to the right or left of the coffin?'

'It makes no difference at all,' replied Nasrudin. 'Just keep well away from the middle.'

L

Life as a Hermit

While Nasrudin was in exile, he lived for a while as a hermit. One day, Tamerlane, who had been separated from his hunting party, stumbled into a clearing and found the Mulla's ramshackle hut. Nasrudin immediately offered the ruler his supper, which consisted of roast snake and murky water. Tamerlane, starving, accepted the food gratefully. When he had eaten his fill, he wiped his beard and turned to his host.

'How can you bear to have fallen so low that you have had to replace the rich robes of a courtier with rags such as those, and the glorious banquets with snake and water that's hardly fit to drink?'

'Because,' explained the Mulla, 'here all that I see is mine. There are no oppressors such as yourself, and none of your servants such as the executioner, the torturer and the tax-gatherer.'

Literate Animals

The mayor came to visit Nasrudin and, while his host was preparing a meal, he went through the Mulla's letters and private papers. Peeking through the screens between the kitchen and reception room, Nasrudin saw what the mayor was doing but said nothing.

Next day, the mayor sat in the congregation as Nasrudin gave his sermon. 'God truly works in mysterious ways. Now he has given dumb animals the mental capacity to read.'

'What's this?' barked the mayor. 'Are you saying that all animals are literate?'

'Not all,' replied the Mulla, 'just the one that went through my correspondence yesterday.'

L

Literate Donkey

The King grew tired of Nasrudin's habit of bringing his donkey with him to Court.
'From this day on,' he ruled, 'no illiterate may show his face in my presence. Unless you can teach your donkey to read, Mulla, I command you to keep him out of the palace.'

For three weeks Nasrudin appeared before the King without his beast, but at the end of this time he arrived and led the animal up to the royal throne.

'Is your mind so feeble that you have already forgotten my decree?' bellowed the King.

'With your permission, Sire, I will demonstrate that this donkey can read.'

In need of a little entertainment, the monarch gave his consent. Whereupon Nasrudin produced the Qur'an and placed it on the ground in front of the donkey. Sure enough, the animal leafed through the pages with his tongue and, reaching the end of the Holy Book, the creature began to bray loudly.

'I trust Your Majesty is satisfied,' said the Mulla.

'Not until you tell me how you performed this miraculous act,' demanded the Sovereign.

'It was easy,' said Nasrudin, 'I trained my beast by covering each page with oats. Each time I offered him the book, he ate the oats and turned the page in search of more. After three weeks, he has come to associate the Qur'an with food. Now he brays because, for all his licking and searching, he cannot find his meal.'

'This exercise proves nothing!' replied the King.

'Forgive me, Majesty, but I must disagree: it proves that one can teach any dumb animal to read.'

L

Live Long and Prosper

When Tamerlane found his treasurer guilty of embezzlement, he had him executed and engaged Nasrudin as the man's replacement.

But it was not long before a palace aide informed the King that his new appointee was distributing money to the poor. Much enraged, the ruler summoned the treasurer.

'Do you want to end up swinging from the scaffold like your predecessor?'

'Surely you would not hang a man who is simply trying to lengthen your stay on Earth,' replied Nasrudin.

'How will robbing my coffers earn me longer life?' asked Tamerlane.

'As I hand money to the poor and needy, I ask them to pray that our esteemed monarch will live long and prosper. If we did not pay for prayers in this way, who would enlist Allah's help in keeping you alive for another day?'

L

Longer Days

When Nasrudin was a schoolboy, his teacher was greatly interested in life on Earth. He would often speak to the class about nature, detailing the changing of the seasons, the passage of time, and describing how day became night. In one such discussion he said:

'It is spring now and the days are lengthening, while the nights are getting shorter. A month from now — when it's summer, the day will have become longer by an hour.'

Nothing more was said, but a month further into the year, class discussion returned once again to the issue of time.

'Tell us, Nasrudin,' said the teacher, 'how many hours are there in the day?'

'That's easy,' replied the pupil without hesitation. 'Now that it is summer the day is twenty-five hours long. But for the rest of the year the day goes back to being only twenty-four hours.'

L

Look and See

'Tell me, Nasrudin,' said a brutal and unenlightened king, who had heard of the Mulla's powers, 'they say you consort with the Devil. What does he look like?'

'Take a look for yourself, Sire,' said Nasrudin, handing the ruler a mirror.

L

Losing One's Head?

Nasrudin and his friend were out walking when they saw a wolf. The animal darted across their path and then disappeared down a hole. Nasrudin's friend decided to try and dig the animal out. He put his head in the hole and tried to crawl in after the wolf. But the hole was too small, and soon he had become wedged in its opening. Nasrudin watched his friend wriggle and squirm, clearly in terrible distress. After considerable tugging on the Mulla's part, he managed to free his friend. When he looked closer, however, he realised that the man's head was missing. Lifting him onto his shoulder, Nasrudin took him home to the friend's wife:

'Did you happen to notice whether your husband had his head with him when he left the house this morning?'

L

Lost Donkey

asrudin ran into town in a panic. 'Has anyone seen my donkey? If the judge finds it before I do, then I'm a ruined man!'

'Steady on,' said the onlookers. 'If the judge does find the donkey, at least you will know that it is safe and sound and will be returned to you.'

'Safe!' barked the Mulla. 'If the judge does find it he will expect a reward, then he will fine me for having let it escape, then for the donkey trespassing on his property, and then he will fine me for any damage. By the time I get the animal back, all that will be left will be its tail and ears.'

L

Lucky Escape

Nasrudin became so hot when chopping wood that he took off his turban and put it on a wall overlooking the valley below. Seconds later, an eagle swooped down and carried off the fabric.

'What a lucky escape!' stammered the Mulla. 'A few seconds later and I, too, would have been carried off by the bird.'

Lying Low

One day, Nasrudin took some tools to the blacksmith for repair. When he went to collect them, however, the man said they had disappeared. With his old tools gone and no money to buy new ones, Nasrudin had no choice but to ask his neighbour to lend him some.

'Where are your own tools?' asked the man.

'The blacksmith was repairing them, but they disappeared.'

'Then he has certainly stolen them. Go and demand that he return them at once.'

'I cannot. I am avoiding him.'

'Why?'

'Because I have not yet paid him for the repair of my tools.'

Magician or Locksmith?

'Nasrudin,' said the King, 'you are said to be a great magician. I order you to open this priceless jewel box with magic, for it is too valuable to break and holds too many gems to discard.'

'Majesty,' replied Nasrudin, 'you have been misled. I may be a magician, but I am certainly not a locksmith.'

M

Manners cannot be Disguised

*N*asrudin was visiting Samarkand during the reign of Tamerlane — the Ruler of the World. New to the city, he became lost in its back streets and soon found himself in a poorly-lit sector, littered with debris and vacant properties.

'Allah, protect me from the thieves and cut-throats who certainly rule these streets,' he prayed, leading his donkey through the dingy alleys.

By chance, he rode past the Conqueror Tamerlane who, fearful of civil unrest, had donned the disguise of a tramp and was shuffling through the city's most depressed areas in search of rebel rabble-rousers.

Seeing the ragged Mulla, he immediately barred his way. 'How dare a peasant such as yourself ride through this city as if you own the place!' And for good measure he gave Nasrudin a stroke of his whip.

'Dismount at once or your donkey will be confiscated and you shall be beheaded.'

'Great Tamerlane,' faltered Nasrudin, 'have mercy, this animal is the last of my worldly possessions.'

'By the Prophet!' shouted Tamerlane, 'Is my disguise so poor that even a traveller such as yourself can identify me?'

'It was not your costume, but your manner that gave

M

you away,' replied the Mulla. 'A man who commands a complete stranger to dismount on pain of death could be none other than the conqueror responsible for the slaughter of the innocent.'

M

Many Ways to Kill a Tiger

*I*n India, Nasrudin came face to face with a gigantic tiger. Terrified, he scrambled into a tree to hide, but the animal sprang into the branches after him. Trembling with fear, the Mulla climbed higher and higher. The tiger followed with ease. When Nasrudin had reached the highest branch he turned towards the predator and prepared to die. At that moment the tiger saw a fat bird perched to one side and pounced, but the branch on which the bird was sitting was too thin to support the great beast's weight. It snapped and the tiger fell to the ground.

Several hours later, Nasrudin plucked up enough courage to climb down from the tree, and found that the tiger had been killed by the fall. Removing the striped skin, he wrapped it around his shoulders and continued on his way. From that day on, Nasrudin was known as a great hunter.

M

Master and Servant

*T*he sun was going down and it was time for the evening prayer. Nasrudin, who was hurrying home to his son's first birthday party, dashed into the mosque to pray. Catching sight of the hasty worshipper, the Imam crept up and struck Nasrudin hard on the head.

'How dare you offer such slap-dash prayers? Start again, and this time do them differently.'

The Mulla had no choice but to go through the prayers again.

When he had finally finished, the Imam said, 'That's better. I am sure that God appreciated this display of faith far more than the hurried prayers you gave at first.'

'I very much doubt it,' replied Nasrudin. 'Hurried as they were, the first prayers were offered for fear of the wrath of God. The second lot were offered for fear of the wrath of a servant of God.'

M

Meditation

Nasrudin was once disciple to a Sufi Master. One summer afternoon the teacher instructed his pupils to repeat a series of chants designed to induce a meditative trance. The rhythm of the words and the warm sunshine soon caused Nasrudin to doze off.

'How do you manage to enter such a deep meditative state,' the pupils next to him asked after the exercise was over.

'The secret,' replied Nasrudin, 'is learning to sleep with your eyes open.'

M

Melon or Mountain?

As a youngster, Nasrudin was forever getting into mischief. One day, he spotted the mayor of the town strutting by with a turban as big as a boulder. Nasrudin snatched up a rock and hurled it at the dignitary's head-gear. The stone hit the mayor smack between the eyes. Incensed, he marched the naughty boy home.

'Explain yourself!' demanded his father.

'Forgive me,' replied Nasrudin. 'I saw our honoured mayor's turban and thought a man of such stature surely had a head as solid as a mountain. How was I to know that it is really as soft as a melon?'

M

Misjudged

Nasrudin became so irritated by his bad-tempered goose that he took her to the bazaar to sell.

'I'll sell that fine goose for you,' said a broker, eagerly.

'Actually,' replied Nasrudin, 'the goose is far from fine. It hisses and flaps its wings in the most menacing way. I have come to dislike it intensely.'

Begging the Mulla to refrain from saying any more, in case he deterred prospective buyers, the broker ushered him to a nearby teahouse.

'Wait here, and when I have made the sale, I will bring you your share.'

As the Mulla sat drinking tea he heard the broker exclaim: 'Who will give me a fair price for this beautiful, plump goose. To be sure, I have never seen such a sweet-tempered bird.'

Hastily, Nasrudin returned to the auction and stopped the sale. Tucking the goose under one arm, he addressed it apologetically: 'How I have misjudged you! Let's go home.'

M

Missing Saddle-bags

While Nasrudin was travelling with a caravan, he realised that he had confused his saddle-bags with another trader's. Riding up to the leader of the convoy he whispered in his ear. Immediately the caravan was signalled to halt.

'It has come to my attention that thieves have got to our possessions during the night!' announced the lead man.

The worried traders immediately unloaded their packs to check if anything was missing. With the contents of each load spread on the ground, Nasrudin was easily able to identify his missing bags.

M

Mistaken

Nasrudin wanted to buy a new cooking pot. He went to the ironmonger's, but the ironmonger was asking far too much for his goods.

'I thought this was an ironmonger's, but I must be mistaken,' said Nasrudin. Annoyed, the shop-keeper decided to call Nasrudin's bluff.

'Yes, you are mistaken. The ironmonger's is next door. I sell livestock.'

'Really?' replied the Mulla. 'Business must be booming.'

This time it was the ironmonger who was surprised. 'Why do you say that?'

'If you sell livestock, I would expect the place to be full of all sorts of animals, but all that seems to be left is one mangy old goat.'

M

Money for his Funeral

When Nasrudin's miserly employer refused to pay him his salary, he sat in front of the mansion gates and waited. Several days passed, and eventually the miser noticed the Mulla.

'What are you waiting for?'

'I am waiting to be paid.'

'You will starve to death before I pay you.'

'That is why I am waiting here. Hopefully I will die soon, and the whole town will see that it was your meanness that killed me.'

'Ah, but then I will throw you an extravagant funeral and the people will marvel at my generosity.'

'A lavish funeral sounds good. Give me the money, and I will go and arrange it now.'

The miser handed over the money and Nasrudin hurried off with an amount far greater than the salary he was owed.

M

Monkey in Court

Nasrudin and some of the villagers were gathered around a camp-fire listening to the tall tales of a camel driver.

'I have travelled for many years, to some of the most remote lands. In one, I found monkeys which were so human that it was easy to mistake them for men. The only difference was that they had no powers of logic or reason.'

'So that is how the judge does it!' exclaimed Nasrudin. 'I have long realised that he was inhuman, but couldn't work out how he managed to don such a convincing disguise.'

M

Multiple Questions

*H*earing that Nasrudin's saddle-bags had been stolen, his friends and neighbours came to sympathise. In accordance with the traditions of hospitality, the Mulla invited them in to dine. He provided pulao to so many that the cost of the food far exceeded that of the missing bags. After several days of receiving the guests and their condolences, Nasrudin tired of their endless questions.

'Tell me, Mulla,' said one, 'was there one thief or several?'

'Did they break into the house or did they have a key?' asked a second.

'What time of the night did they come?' asked a third.

'I would answer your questions if I could,' replied the exasperated Mulla, 'but unfortunately I was not part of their gang.'

Mustapha, Ruler of the World

While Nasrudin was Court astrologer, the Grand Vizier's wife came to ask about her unborn child.

'You will bear a son,' announced Nasrudin looking at the stars. 'He will be named Mustapha and will become the next great ruler of Western Asia!'

Much pleased, the woman hurried off to tell her husband. Some months passed, and the woman did indeed give birth to a son, whom she immediately named Mustapha. But three days later the baby died. When the distraught woman informed the King, he ordered Nasrudin to appear before him.

'You have lied to the wife of the Grand Vizier and will be banished from this Court forever!'

'Majesty,' replied the astrologer, 'have mercy! All I told was the truth. How can I be held responsible for the time the Angel of Death selects to carry mortals to the other world?'

M

Mutual Gain

asrudin was employed by a merchant to transport a chest containing a thousand gold pieces from one town to the next. On the way, he was attacked by a band of fierce brigands, who stole the money and rode off into the mountains. Battered and bleeding, Nasrudin made his way to the palace to complain:

'Your Majesty! Thanks to the poor policing of the hills, I have been beaten and robbed, and will no doubt be beaten again when my employer hears that I have lost his gold. Return my money to me at once!'

Incensed at being bossed about by a peasant, the King told his guards to throw Nasrudin out of the palace gates. In desperation, the Mulla went to the Mosque:

'Almighty Allah, the King will not hear my pleas, and so I must throw myself on the mercy of one far greater than he. I have been robbed of a thousand gold pieces and beaten twice. Without the money, I will surely be beaten a third time today!'

As he left the mosque, a merchant tapped him on the arm:

'I have just returned from a trading trip which took me across the Hindu Kush. At the summit of one majestic peak, my pony stumbled and I was thrown down the slope. As I fell, I prayed to God for assistance and

M

promised that, should I live, I would give a thousand pieces of gold to the first needy man I met. Just then, a sapling caught my cloak and I was able to find a foothold and climb back to my mount unscathed. I could not help overhearing your prayer, just now, and ask you to accept a gift of a thousand gold pieces.'

Nasrudin was amazed:

'First, Allah had thieves deprive me of a thousand gold pieces, then He threw an innocent man over a cliff so that He would beg to give a stranger a thousand gold pieces. And, finally, He engineered things so that we two could meet for mutual gain.

'I had no idea He took our prayers so seriously.'

M

Mutual Respect

'Hey, Nasrudin!' called the Mulla's wife, 'we must hurry or we will be late for the mayor's funeral.'

'Why should I bother to attend his funeral?' replied her husband. 'He certainly won't trouble to come to mine.'

M

My Back Told me

One day, the King learnt that a local judge had pardoned three petty criminals. He immediately summoned the unfortunate official and told his guards to beat him with his own belt. After a number of ferocious lashes, the poor man died from his wounds.

Nasrudin was made his replacement. From that day on, he appeared in the court-house wearing a belt of feathers. When he was asked why he had chosen this unusual accessory, he smiled.

'It was my back's idea. It told me that it prefers tickling to whipping.'

M

My Burden

Nasrudin was passing the horse auction when the auctioneer rushed up and seized his donkey, which he then attempted to lead to the rostrum. The ass refused to move. A second broker tried to inspect the donkey's teeth and was bitten on the hand. A third reached to examine the donkey's hooves and was kicked in the stomach.

'How do you expect to find a buyer for such an evil-tempered beast!'

'I am not here to sell him,' replied Nasrudin. 'I brought him here to show everyone how difficult he is to get on with.'

M

My Donkey's Idea

Nasrudin knocked on the Imam's door. 'You have come to visit me!' grunted the Imam.

'Actually, it was my donkey's idea,' replied Nasrudin. 'He thought it was time we called on one of his friends for a change.'

M

My Enemies

One day, Nasrudin was listening to a general as he prepared for battle.

'I will tear out the hearts of my enemies. Rip out their tongues. Sever their heads and place them on pikes for all to see!'

'Why not practise on your tongue first?' said the Mulla. 'And then we won't have to listen to any more of your boasting!'

M

My Master's Importance

The judge employed Nasrudin as his coachman. One day, he was driving his master to court when another carriage blocked their way.

'Get out of the road!' the Mulla shouted at the other vehicle's driver.

'How dare you order me about?' replied the other coachman. 'I am the servant of the most important man in town!'

'And who do you think I am servant to?' shouted Nasrudin, 'a goat?'

M

My Wife's Money

The bailiffs had stripped Nasrudin's house bare, but he still owed the state five hundred pieces of gold. The King sent word bidding him to come to the palace and repay the debt.

'I have nothing left to give, Majesty. The only money left is five hundred gold pieces, but that belongs to my wife.'

'According to law, your wife's possessions are your own. Go home and collect the gold.'

'I cannot do that, Majesty,' replied the Mulla, 'because that money is her dowry which I haven't yet paid.'

M

Naked Truth

When Nasrudin was young, he liked nothing better than to sit around the camp-fire listening to stories of distant lands. One day, a caravan of merchants arrived in town. As they ate the evening meal they told of their adventures in foreign parts: of bandits and feats of great daring, of hostility and hospitality, and of strange and wonderful sights.

'We have been through some extraordinary countries,' said a silk merchant. 'Many months' journey from here, we found ourselves in a land so hot that people walked about completely unclothed.' At this revelation, an appropriate hush fell over the audience. Nasrudin broke the silence.

'This could not possibly be! For without clothes, it must have been impossible to distinguish woman from man.'

Nasrudin Dies

Once, Nasrudin fell ill and his wife called the doctor. Giving the Mulla a cursory examination, the doctor announced:

'My friend, I can do nothing for you. Prepare to be taken from this world by the Angel of Death.' With this, he asked for fifty pieces of gold as his fee and left the house.

Several weeks passed, and Nasrudin began to recover his strength. Some time later, haggard and drawn from his past illness, he was walking in the bazaar when he met the doctor.

'You have returned from the dead!' shrieked the man in alarm. 'Tell me, what is it like?'

'Very tiring,' replied Nasrudin. 'The Angel of Death and his helpers spend their whole time deciding who to take next.'

'When will my time come?' asked the terrified physician.

'Interesting that you should ask,' replied Nasrudin. 'Only the other day, they were saying that all doctors should be taken to Hell because they cure people and stop the angels doing their work. But don't worry! I told them that you were incapable of curing anyone and, thus, would do nothing to stand in their way.'

N

Nasrudin's Parrot

Nasrudin dreamt that he owned a rare bird. When he awoke, he said to his wife: 'In my dreams, I owned a splendid parrot that was the envy of the whole town.'

'What a shame that you don't,' replied his wife, 'for if you really did own such a prize, I would teach it to speak and soon it would be the envy of the whole kingdom.'

'And the King would hear of it and offer us a thousand gold pieces for it!' wept the Mulla.

'And then you could dream up a replacement, and we could be even richer. Until finally, you would be King and I would be Queen!'

'But what if the bird learnt rude words and instead of rewarding us, the King ordered our deaths?' asked Nasrudin.

'If it did that, I would take an axe and chop its head off!'

Nasrudin was outraged:

'You would kill a bird that could earn our fortunes?' he snorted, slapping his wife. Hearing the poor woman's screams, the neighbours arrived.

'How dare you attack a helpless woman!' exclaimed the neighbour's wife.

'Helpless?' screamed the Mulla, 'A moment ago, she was strong enough to murder our parrot!'

N

Nasrudin's Shoes

One day, Tamerlane tired of his usual amusements and devised a new game. Nasrudin was forced to stand in front of the Emperor's archers and act as a human target.

Trembling in his shoes, Nasrudin stood motionless as each soldier aimed and fired. Arrow after arrow pierced the Mulla's turban and coat sleeves. But the King's bowmen were so skilled that not a single arrow injured the sage.

When the contest was over, Tamerlane bid his servants replace the target's holed coat and turban with garments from his own wardrobe.

'Please also ask them to bring a pair of your shoes,' said Nasrudin, 'for my own have turned to dust.'

N

Nasrudin's Unruly Sandal

Nasrudin put on one of his sandals after leaving the mosque and was just reaching for the second when a juvenile snatched it away. When the Mulla tried to get the sandal back, the youngster laughed and threw it to his friend. Each time the Mulla made a lunge for the sandal, it flew over his head and into the hands of the other boy. No amount of cajoling, threats or bribes would induce the two to return the sandal to its owner. Finally Nasrudin tired of the game and started to hobble home. On the way back he met his neighbour.

'Mulla, why are you only wearing one sandal?'

'Because the other decided to stay in town and play with its young friends.'

Natural Layout

'Father,' asked Nasrudin's young son, 'why do you say so little and listen so much?'
'Because I have two ears and only one mouth.'

Natural Skill

Nasrudin's baby routinely woke his parents up with his crying. On the third sleepless night in a row, the Mulla's wife turned to her husband: 'Is there nothing you can do?'

'I have tried every trick I know. I am afraid that the only man with the skills necessary to send the child to sleep is the Imam.'

'But he does not even have children of his own. What will he know that we do not?'

'It is not a matter of knowledge but of natural skill. I have seen a whole congregation start snoring the moment he opens his mouth.'

N

Nature's Blanket

*T*ime and again, Nasrudin was kept awake by his wife's moaning about his laziness. 'Oh, what an idler I have for a husband.' she whined one night.

'Since we've been married I've been poor — and thanks to you I'll die poor too. We cannot even afford a decent blanket on your miserable earnings.'

Nasrudin jumped up and ran into the garden. Two minutes later, he returned with a blanket full of earth.

'What do you think you are doing, bringing mud into the house in the middle of the night?' screeched his wife.

'Earth that's good enough to cover our ancestors is good enough to cover you,' replied Nasrudin. 'I haven't heard them complaining about the cold since they have lain beneath it.'

N

Never Born

While in India, Nasrudin visited a huge cemetery. Stopping in front of one elaborate tomb he read:

'Here lies the greatest ruler this land has ever known. He led his armies into battle against enemy forces. He built schools and housing for the poor. His bravery and charity made him a legend in his own lifetime. This noble ruler died aged five.'

'How could a ruler possibly have achieved so much in such a short time?' Nasrudin asked the attendant at the tomb.

'The Sultan came to the throne aged twenty and ruled for the sixty years. On his deathbed, aged eighty, he declared:

'"I have spent seven years studying, eight years at war and sixty years worrying about affairs of state. In all, I have lived five years of my life. This is the age I want recorded on my headstone."'

'If that is how age is estimated here,' said Nasrudin, 'please see that these words appear on my epitaph:

'"Here lies Nasrudin, a man who was never even born!"'

N

Never Satisfied

Nasrudin was out riding when his donkey saw some manure and stopped to inspect it. With much muttering, the Mulla dismounted, scooped up the manure in a nosebag, climbed back onto the donkey and continued on his way home. When they arrived, Nasrudin hooked the nosebag over the donkey's head and went into the house. Soon, the animal began stamping and kicking and tossing its head.

Hearing the commotion, Nasrudin came running back out.

'Are you never satisfied? You wanted that manure, and now you have it to sniff at your leisure you decide you no longer want it!'

N

Next Time

One night, a thief broke into Nasrudin's house and stole the blanket from his bed. 'What are you waiting for?' asked his wife. 'Chase the scoundrel and retrieve our blanket.'

'I will tackle him when he comes back for the bed,' said Nasrudin.

Night Blindness

Nasrudin called the doctor and complained of black spots before his eyes. By the time the physician had examined him and written out the prescription, night had fallen, and he asked to borrow a lamp. Some days later, he met Nasrudin and enquired about his sight.

'Unfortunately,' said Nasrudin, shaking his head, 'I now suffer from total night blindness. Perhaps that is because you still have my lamp.'

N

Nobody's Fool

Nasrudin was forever being teased by his classmates, who thought him something of a simpleton. One day, one of his peers picked up an old boot from the street and asked Nasrudin what it was.

'Can you not see for yourself?' he replied. 'It is obviously the cover for a boot-shaped scythe.'

N

No Consideration

$\mathcal{N}$asrudin rushed home one evening and called his wife.

'I have invited the judge and his wife for supper and they will be arriving any moment! Go and bake some pies.'

'You never consider me,' grumbled his wife. 'I have spent the whole day cleaning and I am exhausted. And anyway, we have very little flour left.'

'Then make the pies very small,' replied Nasrudin.

N

No Ears, no Crime

One day, the judge asked Nasrudin to help him solve a legal problem.

'How would you suggest I punish a slanderer?'

'Cut off the ears of all who listen to his lies,' the Mulla replied.

N

No Good for my Health

The Imam, an old man who was looking forward to a comfortable retirement, decided to add to his savings. One evening, after prayers, he called the pious to follow him into the graveyard.

'Each of you is to choose the plot of land in which you wish to be buried,' he instructed. 'Give me fifty gold pieces, and I shall note your preferences in this book.'

After much debate and inspection, all present had selected a site of rest except for Mulla Nasrudin.

'If you don't make your mind up soon,' the Imam warned, 'there will be nowhere left for your grave.'

'Thank goodness for that!' replied the Mulla. 'Cemeteries are not good for my health. They always make me think of death.'

N

No Need for Brains

One day, the King fell ill and the best surgeons in the land were called for. One of them, arriving from the sophisticated city of Baghdad, examined the ruler, opened his skull, removed his brain and extracted a large tumour. But it was only when he had replaced the top of the monarch's head that he realised that he had forgotten to include the remains of his brain.

'I shouldn't worry too much,' said Nasrudin, who was among the physicians who had been summoned. 'He just has to sit in state as he did before. His policies will not change, but we will need to find him a bigger turban.'

No Room for More

asrudin and his brother pooled the last of their money and bought some meat and rice in the bazaar. They made a pulao and sat down to eat. After they had each taken a few bites, Nasrudin's brother complained:

'Why is it that, when you reach out for food, you take two pieces of meat each time?'

'I know,' replied Nasrudin. 'It's because I can only fit two pieces in my hand at a time.'

N

No Such Thing as a Free Lunch

Nasrudin was returning from a trip to Bombay when he saw the village judge tucking into a huge picnic by the side of the road.

Approaching the notable, he took a seat beside the hamper and waited to be invited to join the feast. The judge munched on silently for a few moments and then asked Nasrudin about his travels. Hoping that good news might induce the judge to share his meal, Nasrudin began:

'While in India I met your son, who asked me to send his respects and the news that your goat herds are flourishing.'

'Splendid, I am delighted to hear that both boy and goats are well. Tell me, what is my son up to?'

'He's training your white mare to trot.'

'So, the horse is in good health too.'

'Yes, your wife seems to think so.'

'You saw my wife as well?'

'She offered to introduce me to her uncle who is currently looking for new business partners.'

'It is always a pleasure to hear good tidings about one's family,' said the judge, removing the napkin from his collar and starting to pack up the remains of the food.

'Let me repay you for your cheering words. Take any of these scraps and eat your fill,' and he passed the Mulla a few crusts of bread and chicken bones.

N

Fuming at the man's lack of generosity, Nasrudin hissed:

'Not even your goats — had they survived the drought — would have eaten these!'

'I thought you said that the herd was well?'

'It was fine until your son rode off on your mare and left your wife to tend the herd.'

'But why did she let them die?'

'She was herself weakened by the heat. She struggled on valiantly for several weeks, but eventually she met the same fate as the goats.'

'And why has her uncle not contacted me?'

'Apparently he embezzled money from his company in order to pay for your wife's funeral. The theft was discovered and he was thrown into jail.'

Much shaken, the judge sprang onto his thoroughbred and rode off, leaving the hamper and its tasty contents lying by the roadside.

N

Not a Question of Age

Nasrudin was invited to go hunting with some friends. As he had no hunter of his own, he was lent a large mount for the day. The animal's back was so high that, try as he might, he could not get up onto the saddle.

'I am getting old!' he laughed to cover his embarrassment. Then, seeing that the other riders had gone on without him and he was alone, he added:

'Although I was never very supple as a young man either.'

N

Nothing to Do with Me

asrudin joined a caravan picking its way through the desert. On the evening of the first day's travel, the convoy stopped outside a small town. The Mulla turned to the camel man beside him and said:

'Take this money and buy something for our supper. I must light the camp-fire.'

'That has nothing to do with me,' replied the lazy man, sitting himself down.

Nasrudin lit the camp-fire, then trekked into town, bought some provisions and returned to the camp site. In his absence, the other man had allowed the fire to go out. 'Build up the fire,' he said to the idler, 'I have this goat to skin.'

'That has nothing to do with me,' replied the other, wrapping himself up in a blanket.

Nasrudin built up the fire and went to prepare the goat. When the meat was ready to be cooked, he turned to the camel man again: 'Turn the spit while I discuss some business with the other merchants.'

'That has nothing to do with me,' replied the man once again.

Nasrudin placed the goat over the fire and cooked it. Then he hurried off and asked the merchants to join him for supper so that they could conclude their business.

When the guests had seated themselves around the fire and taken their share of the meat, the lazy camel man came for his supper.

'Hey!' he complained, 'there is no goat left!'

'That has nothing to do with me,' said Nasrudin.

N

No Time for Clothes

Nasrudin was sitting in the Turkish baths in Istanbul, when he heard that a man from his village was about to make the long journey home. Leaping up, he rushed naked out of the baths, down the street and clambered onto the back of the cart. Several weeks later, the travellers finally reached their destination.

The whole village had heard of their return and had assembled in the main square to greet them. When Nasrudin sprang from the cart, his family was horrified to see that he was completely naked.

'Where are your clothes?' they asked faintly.

'When I heard that the cart was leaving, I was so sure that you would be pleased by my return that I did not waste valuable time getting dressed.'

N

No Time to Grieve

When Nasrudin's donkey fell ill, the Mulla burst into tears.

'Why are you crying?' asked his neighbour. 'The poor beast is still alive.'

'But if he does die, I will have to bury him, then save for a new donkey, then go to the donkey auction, and then train the replacement. I will have no time to grieve.'

N

Not in Stock

A man came into Nasrudin's grocery store and asked the price of walnuts

'Two gold pieces per pound.'

'That is a scandalous price!' barked the customer. 'Do you not have a shred of conscience?'

'I am sorry,' replied the Mulla, 'but I don't have such commodities in stock.'

N

Not until I Say

The villagers finally tired of their Imam. 'Nasrudin,' they beseeched, 'we can't bear to hear his grating voice for another day. Your tones are far more melodious, please come and be the new Imam.'

'You idiot!' said his wife when he told her of his new position. 'Don't you know that the last Imam hadn't a penny to live on because not one of the faithful ever made a donation?'

Before prayers the next day, Nasrudin made an announcement:

'It has come to my attention that some of you rush your prayers in a way which is quite unacceptable. From now on, anyone who raises their head before I do will incur the wrath of God. His livestock will die of disease. His business will collapse and his house will be swallowed up by the Earth.'

He then began to lead the congregation in prayer. When the time came, he bowed and put his forehead on the ground. The worshippers followed suit. Several hours later, the Imam had not moved and, fearing the wrath of Allah, no member of the congregation dared lift his head before signalled to do so.

As night fell, one man couldn't stand the discomfort

N

any longer:

'Respected Imam,' he said, 'our necks are ready to snap and our foreheads are quite bruised. Couldn't you raise your head?'

'Only if you pay a donation,' replied Nasrudin. 'If not, Allah expects me to prostrate myself for several years.'

One by one, the men reached in their pockets and paid their dues.

'Now,' said Nasrudin, 'anyone who wants to raise their head may do so when he has paid in advance for the next three years.'

Again, the worshippers had no choice but to hand over their money. When everyone had paid, Nasrudin straightened up.

'From now on,' he declared, 'you may bow and raise your heads whenever you like.'

N

No Witnesses

A tramp was making his way along the riverbank when he discovered an iron casket buried in the muddy bank. Retrieving and opening it, he found it contained a considerable amount of gold. He quickly sat down and started to count the money.

While he was doing this, a wealthy land-owner rode by. Seeing the gold, he stopped.

'Where did you get that?' he asked.

'I found it on the riverbank.'

'Well, take care, this area is infested with robbers. They will cut your throat and steal your gold. Perhaps I could ride back with you and put the casket in my safe?' Much relieved, the tramp accepted the offer.

When the gold was safely deposited in the vault, the land-owner told the tramp to return in daylight and he would hand over the box. But when he arrived next day the rich man denied all knowledge of the fortune.

Realising that he was not going to get what was rightfully his, the tramp hauled the thief to court, where Nasrudin was, at that time, acting judge.

'Were there any witnesses?' he asked the tramp.

'Alas no!' replied the man, 'I found it by the river while nobody else was around.'

'Then go and order the river to appear in court.' The

N

man was most surprised, but nevertheless he set off to talk to the river.

A few hours later, he had still not returned.

'Do you suppose he will be long?' asked the judge.

'He might be quite some time,' replied the land-owner. 'That stretch of the river is very far away.'

Finally, the tramp returned, hot and annoyed: 'I begged the river to come until I was blue in the face, but it never budged.'

'Yes it did,' said Nasrudin, pointing to the land-owner. 'It popped in while you were on your way back and told me that this man is indeed a thief.'

N

Offensive Explanations

The King decided to test Nasrudin's wit.
'I have thought of a tricky problem for you, Mulla. See if you can offend me in such a way that your explanation will be a hundred times worse than the original faux-pas.'

Nasrudin agreed. Several days later, the two men were out walking when Nasrudin grabbed the King by the beard and kissed him on the mouth.

'What on earth are you doing?' spluttered the horrified monarch.

'Forgive me, Your Majesty,' replied the Mulla. 'For a moment I confused you with your wife.'

Once on Dry Land

Nasrudin and his son were out fishing when a whirlwind appeared on the horizon. 'God,' pleaded the Mulla, 'spare our flimsy craft and I will reward a needy man with a camel the size of a house!'

'Father, how will you find a camel that large?'

'I will worry about that once we are on dry land.'

One Horse, Two Owners

As equerry to the Caliph of Baghdad, Nasrudin was given a purse of gold with which to buy a new stallion for the stables.

Unable to find a suitable mount at the horse auction, he was on his way home when a glittering procession paraded past. At its head rode a bejewelled figure on a snow-white thoroughbred. Nasrudin recognised the rider: he was the ruler of the neighbouring kingdom — a man famous for his good-will towards the common man.

'Majesty,' called the Mulla, 'could a humble peasant such as I dare to request a lift?'

'Certainly,' replied the monarch. 'Jump up behind me.'

As the King and his entourage neared the nearby town, Nasrudin sighed.

'Are you not comfortable?' asked the ruler.

'Quite, Majesty, but I was just thinking how proud my young son would be to see his father ride into town on such a steed as this.'

The King immediately gestured to the convoy to stop so that he and Nasrudin could change places. Thus mounted, the Mulla rode through the gates. When the Caliph saw his equerry arriving on such a desirable mount he was delighted.

'What a good choice!' he called out, stroking the glossy

mane. 'Dismount and let me try the saddle.'

When the visiting ruler refused, the Caliph was most displeased.

'Get off my thoroughbred! Surely you have a steed of your own.'

Soon a fight broke out between the two rulers' guards and in the confusion Nasrudin, and the purse of gold, disappeared.

O

One Little Word

asrudin's wife was called 'Houri', so named after the beautiful maidens who Muslims believe reside with the blessed in Paradise.

When war came to the land, all men were being called to join the army:

'Join up now!' said a recruiting general, 'and follow the King's men into battle. If you are victorious, you can take your pick of the spoils of war... if you die on the battlefield, you will earn a place in eternal Paradise where you can take your pick of the heavenly houris.'

'I already have a houri at home,' shouted Nasrudin from the crowd. 'She might not be a heavenly houri but at least I do not have to suffer the horrors of war, and a painful death, just for one little word.'

One or the Other

asrudin took a sparrow to the King as a present. Feeling in a generous mood, the monarch gave him a gold piece in return. The treasurer was worried by such extravagance:

'Majesty, if you continue to behave in such a generous manner, the coffers will soon be empty!'

The King agreed, but could not think of a way of asking Nasrudin to return the money without looking mean.

'Leave it to me, Majesty,' said the treasurer. 'I will ask Nasrudin if the bird is male or female. If he says it is male, you can say you wanted a female bird, and if it is female, you can say you wanted a male.'

Nasrudin was called back to Court.

'Mulla,' asked the treasurer, 'is the bird you gave the King male or female?'

Guessing the question to be a trick, Nasrudin instantly replied: 'It is a bisexual bird.'

On Foot

When Nasrudin's donkey finally died of old age, he was inconsolable for several days. His wife became so alarmed by his refusals of food and water that she asked the Imam to speak to him.

'Mulla,' began the Imam kindly, 'all of God's creatures eventually die. Remember the mayor's favourite stallion: he lived but three years. And Antar, the tax gatherer's grey mule, passed away after many years of valiant service. Even my own trusty steed succumbed to death a few months ago. And his replacement will also die one day.'

'That is the point!' said Nasrudin. 'All of the men to whom you refer are in a position to buy a new mount. When I die, I will go to join my donkey in Heaven on foot.'

O

Only One Prophet

One day, Tamerlane turned to one of his guests and asked:

'Who is your mentor?'

'You, O Summit of the Globe!' replied the man.

'If I am your mentor, then who is your prophet?'

Before the guest had time to answer, Nasrudin broke in: 'If you are truly his mentor, he can only have one prophet, none other than the ogre Genghis Khan himself!'

O

On my Mother's Behalf

Nasrudin's neighbour noticed that the Mulla often ended his sentences with the words: 'May my late mother stay in Paradise.'
One day, he asked what the words meant.

'It is simple,' replied Nasrudin. 'My father, who has also died, was a very forceful man who always got his own way. My mother, on the other hand, was meek by nature. I always try and put in a good word for her because I know she finds it hard to stand up for herself.'

Outliving Death

Nasrudin and his neighbour were comparing stories of financial ruin.

'You may be poor, Mulla,' said the other man, 'but I owe so much that I shall be unable to repay the amount during my lifetime. My children will soon have to shoulder the burden of my debts and they, in turn, will be unable to pay. And so the debt will remain unpaid until the Angel of Death comes to rip my soul from me.'

'If I were you,' suggested Nasrudin, 'I would stop repayments immediately and hope that the Angel of Death dies first.'

Painful Dreams

Nasrudin's wife turned to him one morning: 'Last night I dreamt that as I was preparing vegetables for a stew, the knife slipped and I cut my finger.'

'Tonight you had better sleep wearing gloves,' replied the Mulla.

Palpitations

'Careful, Nasrudin,' said his miserly host, watching him drain his third bowl of soup. 'They say that too much salty food can cause the heart to palpitate.'

'Your heart or mine?'

P

Paradise is not Far

Before Nasrudin could afford a donkey he had to go everywhere on foot. One day, he was walking into town when some of his pupils rode by in a cart:

'Teacher!' they laughed as the cart rattled by, 'You will take a long time if you have to walk to Paradise!'

A few seconds later, a horseman on a graceful black hunter offered Nasrudin a ride into town. Climbing up behind the noble, the Mulla waved to the students.

'Apparently Paradise is just a few feet off the ground.'

P

Partial Recovery

Nasrudin fell seriously ill and the doctor came to see him.

'I can cure you,' he told the Mulla, 'but the treatment will be very expensive.'

'How much will it cost?' gasped the patient.

'Three sacks of rice.'

Nasrudin agreed to pay when he had recovered. But, as soon as he began to feel a little better, he stopped taking the medicine.

'Do you want to have a relapse?' snapped his wife.

'Partial recovery equals partial payment,' replied Nasrudin.

P

Pastry without Pies

'Take our apricots to the baker and have him make them into pies,' Nasrudin's wife told her husband. The Mulla loaded his donkey with fruit and set off for town. Passing the teahouse, he noticed some men playing cards.

'Come and try your luck, Mulla!' one called.

'I have no money,' replied Nasrudin.

'Then bet your apricots,' came the reply. Feeling lucky, Nasrudin bet his load and lost everything. Determined to recoup the loss, he wagered his donkey. Again he lost, and returned home empty-handed.

'Where are the pies?' asked his wife.

'There was not enough fruit to fill a single pie,' lied Nasrudin.

'Then where is your donkey?' demanded his suspicious wife.

'The baker took the donkey to pay for the pastry,' replied Nasrudin.

P

Payment in Kind

A travelling scholar knocked at Nasrudin's door and asked for a glass of water. Respecting the sacred Eastern obligation of providing water, Nasrudin invited the man in. As soon as he crossed the threshold, the intellectual began a monologue of facts that lasted several hours. During this time, Nasrudin politely served water, tea, supper and confectionery. Finally, the guest seemed ready to leave.

'If you give me something for my words of wisdom, I'll be on my way.'

'Unfortunately I have nothing left to offer. Come back tomorrow and I will have something for you then,' said the Mulla, taken aback.

Next evening, the scholar returned. Nasrudin ushered him straight into the house and sat him down. The Mulla then began to tell stories of his own travels. After many hours had passed, the exhausted and hungry guest said:

'What about my payment? You said that if I returned today you would give me something for yesterday's conversation.'

'I have paid you,' replied Nasrudin. 'I have paid you in kind.'

Peasants and Kings

One day, the King and his hunting party rode into a small village. Much excited by the chance royal visit, the inhabitants gathered in the main square to see the monarch. After a few minutes, a farmer offered the King a cup of water. The ruler snatched the vessel from the ragged man's hand, downed the water in one gulp and ordered his party to move on.

'How sad it is to view such ill manners,' said Nasrudin, riding at the King's side.

'I am surprised, Mulla,' replied the King. 'You usually defend the underdog.'

'I meant your manners, Majesty.'

'My manners are impeccable. Since when has a great man such as I been obliged to thank a peasant for a cup of water?'

'Since the time when, without serfs such as he, there would be no great men such as you.'

P

Peel and All

Nasrudin's wife watched fascinated as her husband ate his oranges, peel and all. 'Are you not forgetting to remove the peel?' she asked as he bit into another piece of fruit.

'The fruit-seller is a very conscientious man,' replied Nasrudin. 'If oranges were meant to be eaten without the peel, he would have removed it before the sale.'

Pen or Axe?

The Emperor of Persia was on his way to the main mosque. Wishing to wipe the perspiration from his brow, he pulled out a beautifully embroidered handkerchief and, in doing so, dropped his golden pen, which rolled away and came to rest at Nasrudin's feet.

'Don't just stand there, man! Pick it up and return it to me!'

'O Majesty,' said the Mulla as he handed back the pen, 'why do you carry this axe with you?'

'You must be even more of an idiot than you first appear,' said the ruler, 'to confuse a pen with an axe.'

'With your signature, you can destroy whole villages,' said Nasrudin, 'so what could your pen be but an axe?'

P

Pheasant Messenger

When Nasrudin became judge, the Imam was mad with rage. He had coveted the position for quite some time. Trying to undermine the new judge's authority, the Imam spread all sorts of rumours around town. Nasrudin knew the lies were circulating, but resolved to say nothing.

One day, a friendly land-owner gave Nasrudin three pheasants. Thanking the man, Nasrudin took one bird and put it into the pot. The second he hid under the stove. Telling his wife to make a sumptuous meal, he tucked the third bird under his arm and went off to visit the Imam.

'How kind of you to visit me,' said the Imam when Nasrudin arrived, and he offered the judge some tea.

'I have come to ask your advice on a very intricate case,' said his guest, sipping his tea.

The Imam, eager to prove himself wiser than the judge, immediately agreed. 'Perhaps we could discuss the matter over supper tonight,' suggested Nasrudin.

'Nothing would give me greater pleasure!'

At this point, Nasrudin pulled the pheasant out from his coat and said to it:

'Go home and tell my wife that the Imam will be our guest tonight. Ask her to lay the table and make some pheasant stew. Tell her we want chilled watermelon too, and fresh salad. You can prepare the vegetables and eat any peelings.' He then released the bird, which flew off and disappeared into the woods.

The Imam was dumbfounded.

'If you expect me to believe that the bird will do all that, then you must take me for a complete fool!'

'I will not reach any conclusions just yet,' replied Nasrudin, 'but, if the pheasant fails to obey my commands, I will resign as judge.'

Two hours later, he and the Imam set out. Arriving at the judge's house, the supper guest was amazed. Boiling on the stove there was a pot of pheasant stew, while on the beautifully laid table there was salad and pulao and, lying on ice, a watermelon.

'But where is your messenger?' he asked in awe.

'Probably hiding under the stove eating carrot peelings,' replied Nasrudin, retrieving the bird.

The Imam was determined to buy the bird from his host.

'I will give you fifty gold pieces for your feathered servant,' he offered.

'I simply couldn't part with him,' answered the judge. 'He is as dear to me as my own son.'

'One hundred gold pieces,' haggled the Imam, thinking how envious his enemies would be if he had such a bird as his servant.

'As your host I cannot refuse,' replied Nasrudin, taking the money and putting the pheasant in a sack.

The avaricious Imam could not wait to show off his new prize. He hurried straight to his brother-in-law's house, where he called upon the whole family to gather round.

With a flourish he pulled out the bird.

'Go home and tell my wife that our relatives will be dropping in for a late supper. Tell her to have pulao, meatballs, salad, vegetables, and lemon sorbet waiting.' He then released the messenger with a flourish.

When the Imam and his kin arrived at his house, they found the place deserted. The stove was cold, there was no sign of the meal and his wife was nowhere to be seen. Much offended, the guests left. The Imam went to see Nasrudin.

'How dare you trick me! Give me back my money at once!'

'In the first place, I never asked you to buy the bird, I sold it to you at your own insistence. Secondly, your orders to the bird may have been misleading. May I ask what you said to it?'

When the Imam had repeated the instructions he had given the bird, Nasrudin smiled.

'I see what has happened,' he said calmly. 'You dispatched the messenger, but did not tell him where you live. He is probably searching the whole country as we speak. And you think you have the necessary intelligence to be a judge?'

P

Pies or Crumbs?

One day, the baker sent Nasrudin to the palace with a cart-load of fresh pies.

'What have you got there?' asked the suspicious guard, poking the load with a stick.

'If you keep poking, I will have crumbs,' replied Nasrudin.

Plans for Expansion

'Friends,' hollered Nasrudin to his neighbours one day, 'who will give me a fair price for my land?'

'But if you sell your land, how will you live, Mulla?' they asked.

'Simple economics,' replied Nasrudin, 'I will use the money to invest in another small patch which I will then add to what I once had. In this way, I'll be expanding my farm!'

∼281∼

P

Poor Conditions

When the Imam visited Nasrudin's new house, he looked at the cramped dwelling and remarked:

'You live in very poor conditions, it is true, but do not despair. The meek are rewarded in death, and you will go to a place where you will live in splendour such as you have not known in this world.'

'That is all very well,' replied Nasrudin, 'but what am I to do with a luxurious grave?'

P

Power of the Prophets

asrudin went to the Imam of the Great Mosque one day and declared:
'I can perform the skills of the prophets and the saints. On my command, the trees will walk down the mountainside and the rivers alter their course to come to me!'

'Prove that you are indeed blessed with the powers of a prophet by commanding that boulder to roll towards you, or pay dearly for your blasphemy!' shouted the Imam.

Nasrudin stretched his arms out to the rock and told it to come to him, but it did not move an inch. Seeing this, the Mulla walked over to where it lay.

'You said you possessed the powers of the prophets, which you appear not to have,' hissed the Imam. 'Prepare to suffer the consequences.'

'My actions are perfectly permissible by Islamic law,' replied Nasrudin. 'Have you forgotten that when the mountain would not go to the Prophet Mohammed, he went to the mountain?'

P

Prayers

A corrupt official had been taken seriously ill. Nasrudin met the man's wife in the bazaar.

'How is your husband?'

'Everyone is hoping that the villagers' prayers will be granted.'

'If that is the case, I am surprised the burial has not yet taken place.'

P

Prayers for Hire

While Nasrudin was still Imam, a rich merchant came to ask his professional opinion.

'Is it true that a believer must pray five times a day?'

'Yes,' replied the Imam, 'once in the morning, twice during the day, once in the evening and once at night.'

'Then I am in an impossible position. In the morning I am still asleep, during the day I have business to attend to, in the evening I like to relax with my friends, and at night I must perform my duties as a husband.'

'I see your point,' replied Nasrudin.

'Perhaps I could hire you to pray for me?' said the man, offering a handful of coins.

'I don't see why not,' agreed the Imam. But just as his visitor was leaving he handed back one coin.

'You gave me five coins, one for each prayer. But, thinking about it, I can only accept four. The morning, day-time and evening prayers are no problem as I'm here anyway, but at night I sleep, too.'

P

Praying for Miracles

Nasrudin stole into a merchant's warehouse and began to fill a sack with his stores. Seeing the light, the merchant came to investigate and found the Mulla.

'I will have you flogged in the village square for this!' he spluttered, grabbing Nasrudin by the scruff of the neck.

'Please do not humiliate me in public,' pleaded Nasrudin. 'This is a private matter between you and me. So punish me yourself.'

'Very well, I will beat you with the very things you have attempted to steal,' replied the merchant, and started to hit Nasrudin with a bag of flour.'

After a few blows, Nasrudin began to pray to God for a miracle.

'Even a miracle will not save you from this bag of flour,' shouted the merchant.

'It is not the flour I am afraid of,' replied the Mulla. 'I've just remembered that I put your axe at the bottom of the sack. I am asking God to turn it into another bag of flour.'

Precociousness

When Nasrudin was a child he was forever asking his father difficult questions. One day, his father became so embarrassed by his inability to answer that he lost his temper:

'Don't you know that precocious children grow up to become complete fools?!' he snapped.

'Father,' replied the young Nasrudin, 'you never told me that you were a child genius.'

P

Present and Correct

When he had money, Nasrudin was fond of giving parties for his friends. One summer, he organised a very grand affair. He hired a band and caterers, and commissioned the town carpenter to build eight large platforms in the garden. These he covered with carpets and cushions. The evening was a roaring success. The guests ate, drank and danced until dawn. Sitting in the garden after the last merrymaker had left, Nasrudin reviewed the night. As he looked around the garden, his delight that the guests had enjoyed themselves turned to fury. No matter how many times he counted the wooden platforms, only seven of the eight remained.

'What sort of hooligan eats my food, dances to my band, and then carries off a platform, complete with cushions and carpets?' snarled the Mulla, pounding the rostrum beneath him. Only when his hand struck the wooden board did he realise that he was sitting on the eighth construction.

P

Preserving the Fish

Nasrudin was crossing the ocean when another passenger turned to him:
'The captain tells me that you have travelled far and wide. So tell me, why is the sea so salty?'
'Because it is regularly sprinkled with salt so that the fish don't go bad,' the Mulla swiftly replied.

P

Price of an Education

*I*n the bustling city of Baghdad, Nasrudin became separated from his donkey. Having searched for the beast for several hours, the Mulla sat down to ponder his fate at a teahouse in the centre of town. Soon afterwards, he noticed that a crowd had gathered near the university.

Upon investigation, the Mulla found his donkey surrounded by a group of scholars.

'Your donkey has wreaked havoc in this honoured seat of learning,' howled the dean. 'You must pay a hefty fine.'

'Surely,' replied Nasrudin, 'I should charge you. I used to have a perfectly well-mannered donkey. Now look at him! After a few hours at this place, he has turned into a delinquent.'

P

Professional Fee

he mayor was trying to fasten his saddle-bags, but each time he positioned the bag it slipped to one side.

'Nasrudin,' he said, as the Mulla walked by, 'you claim to understand everything. How can I solve this problem?' Inspecting the load, Nasrudin saw that one of the bags was full of rice while the other was empty. 'As a scientist,' he said, 'I can see that the laws of physics are working against you.' He then removed the rice and divided it into three equal piles. He put one pile in each of the bags and, sure enough, the load was perfectly balanced.

'Excellent,' said the mayor, 'but what about the third pile?'

'That,' replied Nasrudin, 'is my professional fee.'

P

Quite Possible

Nasrudin's donkey ran away again.

'Has anyone seen her this time?' he asked a group of villagers.

'I saw her presiding over a criminal case in the courtroom,' said a practical joker.

'Now that is quite possible,' said Nasrudin. 'She always listened most attentively when I taught law to my pupils.'

Reading Aloud

'Tell me, Mulla,' asked the Imam, 'have you ever made a mistake while reading the Qur'an?'

'Indeed I have! Once I misread and instead of saying that sinners would go to Hell, I said Imams would go to Hell. And once I made another mistake and thought that the Holy Book said that Imams, rather than the meek, would inherit the Earth.'

'You think that you are as cunning as a fox,' snarled the Imam, 'but, in truth, you are as dim as a donkey.'

'You are right, Imam. As a human being, rather than an Imam, I am neither as cunning as a fox, nor as dim as a donkey.'

R

Real Bravery

Nasrudin was sitting in the teahouse listening to a boastful young man.

'A bear ran up to me and I clubbed it over the head. A tiger sprang from a tree and I wrestled it to the ground. A fire broke out in a neighbouring house and it was I who fought my way in and rescued the neighbour's tiny children. A tidal wave threatened to consume my town and I held back the waters until everyone had escaped. I must be the bravest man of all.'

'Actually,' replied Nasrudin, 'I am.'

The other tea-drinkers were surprised to hear the usually humble Mulla challenging the young fool.

'Why are you so brave?'

'Because I am not afraid when guests come to my house and I have not a grain of rice in the cupboard, a leaf of tea in the pot or a crumb of bread on the plate.'

Reasons for Lament

asrudin sometimes ferried people across the river in his boat. One day, twelve merchants approached him and asked how much he charged for the service. Seeing the men's exquisite coats, he replied:

'One piece of gold each.'

The price was agreed and Nasrudin loaded the merchants into his rickety boat. But the craft was so full that, halfway across the river, one of the passengers lost his footing and fell overboard.

As he was washed screaming downstream, the merchants started to wail. They were surprised to hear Nasrudin also join in the lament.

'We are crying for our lost friend,' they said. 'Why are you crying?'

'For my lost fare,' replied the Mulla.

R

Reckless Salt

One supper time, Nasrudin sprinkled salt into his soup. Watching it dissolve he said: 'You reckless crystals, why did you dive into the soup if you were not waterproof?'

Relayed Messages

Nasrudin, down on his luck, went to the house of a wealthy trader to ask for a job. He explained his business to the doorman, but the trader would not condescend to see him. Instead, he gestured to the footman: 'Go and tell the cook, to tell the kitchen-hand, to tell the stable-boy, to tell Nasrudin that I have no position vacant.'

Hearing this, the Mulla turned to his donkey:

'Donkey, go and tell my wife, to tell our son, to tell the goats to come to this trader's house and destroy his garden.'

➴296➶

Repaid Debt

Nasrudin went to get a haircut. He pocketed the razor on his way out, and left without paying.

'Hey!' the barber shouted after him, 'you owe me for your haircut!'

'Don't worry,' interjected the man in the next chair, 'the Mulla is an honourable man. He will pay eventually.'

Next day, Nasrudin returned and handed the barber a coin.

'Here is the money I owe you,' he said.

Taking the coin, the barber apologised for doubting the Mulla's honesty.

'But there is still the small matter of my razor.'

'Unfortunately,' replied Nasrudin, 'I had to sell that in order to repay my debt to you.'

R

Repeated Words

For many years, the inhabitants of Nasrudin's village had been crippled by high taxes imposed by the country's unscrupulous King. The farmers and traders were obliged to contribute a third of their meagre earnings to the palace coffers.

Nasrudin, then the village Imam, was so angered by the poverty and inequality around him that he delivered a sermon in which he accused the monarch of bleeding the people dry.

Unfortunately, one of the King's spies heard his remarks and rushed off to the Court. Nasrudin was soon arrested and taken to the palace.

'I hear that you have dared to liken me to a leech,' said the King. 'As you doubtless know, insults aimed at the royal personage are rewarded with public flogging and followed by imprisonment.'

'Your Majesty,' replied the Imam, 'I was not insulting you, I was simply repeating what people all over the kingdom are saying.'

Repentant Thief

While Nasrudin was praying in the mosque, a thief made off with his saddle-bags. When he complained to the Imam, he was told:

'A true believer would have had a few holy sayings from the Qur'an in his bag, and the thief, seeing these, would have immediately repented.'

'How strange it is that he did not,' said the irate Mulla, 'for I had a whole Qur'an in my bag!'

R

Rescue, not Theft

Nasrudin was forever thinking up ways of annoying his neighbour, who was a renowned skinflint. One night, he crept into the miser's yard, grabbed a chicken from the coop and made off with it. As he ran, he chuckled with delight at the pain the loss would cause the wealthy, but miserly man. After several yards he began to wonder why the bird was not making a fuss over its abduction. Perhaps it had been suffocated by the thick material of the bag into which he had hastily forced it. Nasrudin stopped and opened the sack, whereupon the chicken poked its head out and began to make a terrible noise.

'Just as I thought,' said the Mulla. 'You are just as sick of my neighbour's greed as I am. This is a rescue rather than a theft.'

R

Respect

One day, the King and Nasrudin had a squabble and the monarch banished him from the Court. 'I do not wish to see your face again until you are prepared to show me some respect!'

A few weeks passed and the King began to miss Nasrudin. He summoned him back to the palace. When the Mulla arrived, he walked up to the throne backwards.

'What nonsense is this?' asked the King.

'I am simply obeying your previous command,' replied Nasrudin.

R

Respectable Gourmets

The King heard that Nasrudin was something of a gourmet.

'Tell me,' he asked, 'which tastes better: roast goat or roast mutton?'

'That all depends on the kitchen in which the meat is prepared,' replied the Mulla. 'Each cook has his own culinary style.'

Hearing this, the King instructed his head chef to prepare two dishes: one of roast goat, the other of roast mutton. These were soon brought and served to the gourmet.

'So, Nasrudin,' said the monarch, 'which do you prefer?'

'Both were excellent, Sire,' answered Nasrudin. 'But I, like any respectable gourmet, could not possibly choose between the two until I have cleansed my palate with some of the chef's sorbet.'

R

Rice, Mice and Children

Nasrudin's employer, a merchant, exclaimed one day:

'Last winter I buried thirty sacks of rice for safe keeping. Yesterday, I unearthed them and found that the whole lot had been eaten by mice.'

'I had a similar problem with ten sacks of your rice too,' said Nasrudin. 'The ten sacks I took from you for safe keeping last year were also eaten.'

'By mice?'

'No, by my children.'

R

Riches or Rice

While Nasrudin was living in a remote mountain settlement, a caravan of traders wandered from the path and stumbled, exhausted and starving, into town.

Seeing the loaded saddle-bags and weakened merchants, the townsfolk decided to murder the men and steal their wares. But, as their spiritual leader, Nasrudin managed to persuade them to spare the travellers. So, grudgingly, the settlers fed and sheltered the merchants and then gave permission for them to continue on their way.

Preparing to leave, the grateful traders offered to reward Nasrudin for intervening on their behalf. He refused the reward, asking only for ten sacks of rice. When the rice had been handed over and the caravan had left town, the settlers started to regret their charitable behaviour. Seething with resentment, they turned on Nasrudin and demanded that he leave the town. He calmly packed his rice and moved into a shepherd's shack on a nearby slope.

Some days later, the cold weather started to move in and the mountain passes were soon blocked by snow and ice.

Having eaten the last of their stores, the townsfolk remembered Nasrudin's rice. Soon they trekked to his shack and humbly asked him to return to town.

Ridiculous Proportions

asrudin overheard an Iraqi boasting about his home town. 'In Baghdad, we have the most gorgeous mosque in the world. It is over a thousand feet long and two thousand feet wide.'

'That is nothing,' replied the Mulla, hoping to silence the boastful man. 'In my town we have a mosque that is ten thousand feet wide and...'

At that moment, a man from Nasrudin's town rode up and joined them. The Mulla hesitated and amended his story:

'...ten feet high.'

'How can you have such an oddly shaped building?' asked the Iraqi.

'Don't ask me,' replied Nasrudin, 'ask my friend here. He is responsible for its ridiculous proportions.'

R

Ripe Apples

A man walking past Nasrudin's house left his shoes at the foot of the Mulla's apple tree. Looking out of the window, Nasrudin cried out to his wife.

'Quick, get me the axe! I must cut down the fruit tree.'

'Whatever for?' asked the woman. 'Given another two weeks, those apples will be ready to eat. Think of all the delicious things I can make out of them for us and the children.'

'Alas!' answered Nasrudin, 'there is no time to wait. If the owner of those shoes is prepared to leave them under the tree before the apples are ripe, who knows what he'll do when the fruit is ripe?'

R

Ruler of the World

---

*T*amerlane was out hunting when night fell. He signalled the party to stop and make camp. As he and a few courtiers sat around the camp-fire, he called on each man to tell a story.

The Emperor started his narrative first. Before he was more than a few words into the story, a burning ember flew from the flames and settled on the ruler's mighty turban.

'Master,' said Nasrudin seeing the smoke curling from the royal head-gear.

'Master!' snapped the King, much annoyed by the Mulla's interruption, 'I am not a mere master, I am the King of Kings, I am the Conqueror of the World, I am the Ruler of the Universe!'

'Please excuse me,' murmured Nasrudin and politely held his tongue.

R

Ruler or Tyrant?

One day, Tamerlane was bored and decided to have some fun with his courtiers.

'What am I,' he asked his astrologer, 'a tyrant or just a ruler?'

'A ruler,' replied the courtier. He was immediately beheaded.

The Emperor turned to a second sycophant:

'Do you also think I am just a ruler?'

'No, Great Emperor Tamerlane, you are the Most Powerful Tyrant in the World!' Once again, the Shah ordered the executioner to take the man away.

Finally, he turned to Nasrudin:

'What do you think I am?'

'You are neither a tyrant, nor just a ruler,' came the reply.

'Explain!'

'Were you a tyrant, you would not ask the question of humble courtiers. And were you just a ruler, you would not punish men for speaking the truth.'

Rumble the Mouse

'What is in this pot?' Nasrudin asked his wife. 'A tiny mouse called Rumble,' replied the woman. 'Do not remove the lid or she will run away.'

When she had left the house, Nasrudin could not resist peeking into the pot to have a look. But, removing the lid, he found the pot contained yoghurt. Laughing at his wife's attempts to keep him from eating between meals, he took a spoon and had soon scraped the pot clean. When all of the yoghurt was eaten, he replaced the lid and put the pot back in the kitchen.

Half an hour later, his stomach began to make the most terrible noises. The rumbles and gurgles became so fierce that Nasrudin was soon groaning in pain. When his wife returned, she found him curled on the floor, clutching his belly.

'What is the matter with you?'

'I couldn't resist taking a look at Rumble and opened the pot, but she scuttled into my mouth and I swallowed her. Now she's living up to her name, and is desperate to get out.'

R

Saint Nasrudin

Nasrudin rushed up into the throne room and threw himself at the King's feet. 'Your Majesty, Allah has made me a saint and told me to take my place at Court!'

'Are you insane?'

'I must be. Why else would I have agreed to be a saint in your Court?'

S

Sandbags

While ploughing his field, Nasrudin unearthed a pot of gold. According to the law, he was obliged to divide the treasure with the judge who would, in turn, contribute the money to the palace coffers. While he was changing his working clothes for those suited to a visit to the Court, his wife replaced the coins with sand. Unaware of the swap, Nasrudin took the pot to the judge.

'Quick, fetch the scales,' he clamoured on entering the court-room.

Sensing wealth, the judge quickly gave the order for the scales to be brought and began piling weights onto one of the trays. Nasrudin emptied the contents of the pot onto the other.

'What is the meaning of this?' asked the judge.

Recognising his wife's handiwork, the Mulla coolly replied:

'I am making sandbags to hold back a section of the river, and needed to weigh the sand in order to be sure I am making them big enough.'

S

Satan's Replacement

'Nasrudin,' glowered the King, 'I hear that you have been saying that when I die I shall go straight to Hell.'

'You have heard correctly, Majesty.'

'Are you not afraid for your life?'

'But, Sire, I was not criticising but complimenting you.'

'How so?'

'I simply announced that Satan is preparing to welcome you to Hell by renouncing his throne and handing it over to you.'

S

Saved Shoes

One night, Nasrudin thought he heard a fox in the garden. Fearing that the animal was after his chickens, he rushed out of the house barefoot and cut his foot on a piece of jagged rock.

'It is lucky I did not have time to put on my shoes,' he said. 'I may have hurt my foot, but I have saved my shoes.'

Secret Seeds

A trader once set up a market stall selling sesame seeds. To each potential customer he offered a few fried seeds to taste. Finding the delicacy much to his liking, Nasrudin bought six packets.

'What do I do now?' he asked.

'Simply take the seeds and sow them,' replied the merchant.

The Mulla returned home with his purchase, fried the seeds and sowed them. Of course, nothing came of them.

'What a trickster!' cried the Mulla. 'And how typical to keep back something of the secret of how to do it.'

S

Self Defence

Nasrudin was crossing a field when a billy goat charged him. With no time to escape, the Mulla stood his ground and struck the animal between the horns with a large rock. The goat dropped to the ground just as its owner ran up.

'You've killed my best goat.'

'I'm sorry, but it was attempting to kill me.'

'Couldn't you have simply struck it on the rump?'

'I could have,' replied Nasrudin, 'but it was not attempting to kill me with its rump, but with its horns.'

S

Sensitivity

Nasrudin returned home from work exhausted. His back ached from loading sacks onto his donkey, his feet burned with blisters, and his skin was scorched by the sun. Sitting wearily at the table he asked his wife why she had not prepared the evening meal.

'You are a selfish man!' she snapped. 'Today, I went first to my friend's house with soup for her sick husband, but the unfortunate man had already died. Then I went to his funeral and then back to his house to help cook for the funeral guests.'

'For a moment,' said Nasrudin, looking at her swollen eyes, 'I thought you had been to a wedding. You usually return in a similar mood.'

S

Sent by God

Nasrudin was sitting by the sea when a wave washed over him and swept his sandals away. 'That wave was sent by God,' said a bystander. 'God, God!' ranted Nasrudin, 'I would take Him to court for the loss of my sandals, but the judge would probably find in His favour.'

Servant and Master

*N*asrudin had just stored the year's harvest of grain in his barn when the tax man came to claim the Emir's share.

'There must be at least a hundred sacks of grain here, which means you owe the palace thirty bags.'

'Nonsense,' replied the Mulla, counting the bags. 'There are only thirty sacks. If you take these, my family will starve.'

The official remained adamant, and signalled to his minions to load the entire contents of the barn onto his cart. In desperation, Nasrudin decided to follow his yield to the palace and make a formal complaint to the Emir.

'Majesty,' he began, 'I have come to lodge a complaint…'

In no mood for protestations, the ruler silenced Nasrudin with a wave of his hand.

'Mulla, look at yourself — a man some six feet tall and still griping like a small child.'

Hearing these words, the Mulla thanked the monarch for his time and begged leave to return home.

'What?!' challenged the King. 'Are you not going to try and make me see reason?'

'What chance would I have?' replied the Mulla. 'If you estimate my height at six feet, then it is clear that your servant, the tax gatherer, has fashioned his estimations on his master's.'

S

Seven Days

While on his travels, Nasrudin stayed with a legendary warlord. His host gave the Mulla permission to remain in his house while he inspected his lands. When the warrior returned one week later, Nasrudin politely asked him about his journey.

'It was the best of my life!' the man replied.

'On Monday, we travelled to a remote town where floods had drowned every last man, woman and child.

'On Tuesday, we journeyed further and came to a city which had been destroyed by its foes. On Wednesday, we continued and arrived at a forest just in time to see the whole place set ablaze by a bolt of lightning. On Thursday, we pressed on and came to a village where we found a mad dog — I naturally told my men to slaughter the inhabitants to stop the spread of rabies. On Friday, we went in search of other disease victims, but found that famine had done our work for us.

'On Saturday, when we were almost home, our horses bolted and crushed several locals under foot. On Sunday, having retrieved our mounts, we continued and just outside this city we found a man hanging from a tree by his neck.'

'How fortunate for this land and all its inhabitants that you were only gone a week!' replied Nasrudin.

S

Sharp Ribs

The King was in a terrible temper. When Nasrudin made some irreverent comment he called the palace guards.

'Throw this insignificant cur under the feet of my largest elephant!'

'O Ruler of the World,' yelped the Mulla, 'you would be better advised to throw the Grand Vizier under the great beast's feet, for I might cause the elephant such pain that your army will be kept from battle and your empire will fall.'

'How is an insect like you going to pain my noble elephant?'

'I am so ill-nourished that my ribs are razor-sharp. Imagine what would happen if one of these pierced the elephant's foot. The Grand Vizier, on the other hand, a well-padded man, is far less likely to splinter.'

Shock Tactics

Villagers often came to Nasrudin with minor ailments, which he was usually able to cure. As a result, he became known as something of a healer.

A miser called Nasrudin to examine his son. He treated the infant, who soon made a full recovery, but when he asked for payment he was thrown out of the house.

Several months later, the miser fell ill. Once again, Nasrudin was called. This time he had the entire family gather around the patient's bedside, and he announced:

'Regretfully, I can offer no cure.'

'But unless his fever breaks he will die!' moaned his wife.

'Very well,' replied Nasrudin, 'open his safe and give me one hundred pieces of gold.'

Fearing the loss of his hoard, the miser immediately broke into a sweat and his fever disappeared.

S

Shoes and Donkeys

Nasrudin arrived in a strange town as night fell and found that he had nowhere to stay. With no friends to visit and no money for a hotel, he decided to sleep in the mosque. Fearing that thieves would steal his donkey if he left it outside, he led the animal inside, tethered it to the mihrab, and lay down.

Next morning, the Imam arrived, removed his shoes and entered the mosque to pray. When he saw the donkey in the house of God, he kicked Nasrudin sharply in the ribs:

'How dare you bring a filthy beast in here? You have offended Allah and sealed your own death-warrant! I will have you hanged in the town-square!'

Seeing the Imam still clutching his shoes, Nasrudin replied:

'I have done nothing that you have not done yourself. You bring your shoes, worth a few pennies, in here for fear that they will be stolen if left outside. I have led in my donkey — worth many times more — for the very same reason.'

S

Simple Arithmetic

Nasrudin was taking his goat to market to sell. 'Are you asking much?' asked his neighbour. 'Two pieces of gold,' replied the Mulla, 'although I bought it for one, and perhaps someone will buy it for three. If you would like it, I could let you have it for less.'

'How much?'

'Well, as we've established, it is worth six, but I could sell it to you for five.'

S

Since becoming a Mulla

Nasrudin was once studying in the library when he found that the books he needed were on a shelf far too high for him to reach. By stacking up a few of the thickest tomes, he found he could finally reach the top shelf. While he was selecting the books he wanted to carry down, the librarian bustled up.

'You are standing on a pile of Qur'ans! Are you not worried about God?'

'I used to be,' replied Nasrudin, 'but since I became a mulla I expect God is more worried about me.'

Sinner for the Evening

Nasrudin was visiting a Christian friend during the fast of Ramadan. At dinner, his host's wife set a roast goose on the table. She and her husband then served themselves large portions and began hungrily to eat. Realising that he was not about to be offered a plate, Nasrudin ripped a leg from the roast and took an enormous bite.

'Mulla,' apologised his host, 'we assumed that as a believer you would be fasting.'

'For food which tickles the palate like this, I am willing to descend to your level temporarily.'

S

Six and Three make Nine

Nasrudin was most surprised when his new wife gave birth to a son three months after they had got married.

'Correct me if I am wrong,' he asked the woman, 'but does it not usually take nine months?'

'Men!' she grunted. 'You never understand such things. Tell me, how long have you been married to me?'

'Three months.'

'And how long have I been married to you?'

'Three months.'

'And what does three and three make?'

'Six.'

'So take six and add it to the months I have been pregnant and you will find that six and three makes nine.'

'How foolish I was to mistrust you.'

S

Small Appetite

Nasrudin was employed as the cook of the Conqueror Tamerlane. One evening, a guest frowned and scooped a fly from his bowl of soup. Outraged, Tamerlane called for the cook.

'I ought to have you hanged for your inattention. There is a fly in that bowl of soup!'

'I fail to see what all the fuss is about, O Conqueror of Heaven and Earth! Surely, a tiny fly cannot drink more than a minute amount of soup.'

S

Soldiers and Weapons

The Emperor's forces were preparing for battle.

'Nasrudin, observe the weapons of my men. See their shimmering armour, their mighty cannons and shining swords.'

'Unfortunately,' said Nasrudin, 'they do not carry the most vital weapon of all.'

'What is that?'

'Courage in their hearts.'

S

Statement and Belief

One day, while he was Imam, Nasrudin forgot the text of his sermon and blurted out: 'Allah created the world in six months!'

Later, a scholar came to correct the mistake:

'The Qur'an states that it took just six days to create the world.'

'Listen, brother,' replied the Mulla, 'you and I know that that is the case, but there is no way that a flock as illiterate as mine is going to believe that!'

Strict Sentences

The town's judge, who had held the position for many years, was interviewing applicants for his replacement.

'How can I be sure you have a sufficient knowledge of the law to pass sentence?' he asked Nasrudin.

'Simple, Your Honour. Just take your place in the dock and I will try you for your past deeds. You will soon see that I have what it takes to sentence a man to imprisonment for the rest of his days!'

S

Strong Teeth

'Heaven is such a sublime place,' intoned the Imam in his sermon, 'that the angels eat golden grapes with emerald seeds.'

'They must have very strong teeth,' shouted Nasrudin from the crowd.

S

Stuck in the Mud

Nasrudin's donkey was stuck in the mud. No matter how hard the Mulla tugged at the beast's bridle, he could not free its hooves.

'Out of the way!' commanded a messenger, galloping up behind Nasrudin.

'Impossible, I am afraid,' replied the Mulla. 'Only donkeys riding good horses could get through this mud.'

S

Successive Tyrants

For several weeks, Nasrudin had not paid his dues to the local land-owner. One day, the nobleman arrived to collect his rent and, finding Nasrudin unable to pay, told his men to take the Mulla's furniture in lieu of payment.

As the tables and chairs were being loaded onto the cart, Nasrudin fell to his knees and started to pray:

'Merciful Allah, please grant the master of these men eternal life!'

'Is your sarcasm intended to anger me even more?' enquired the noble.

'The sentiment comes from the heart,' replied Nasrudin. 'When your father was still alive, every man in the village prayed for his early demise. But when you became Lord and proved to be a thousand times more oppressive than he, we saw sense. Now we ask God to make you live forever. Who's to say that your successor will not turn out to be a thousand times worse than you?'

S

Sugar Coins

When the Shah-in-Shah heard that a local governor had been embezzling taxes meant for the palace coffers, he sent his troops to visit the man and force a thousand gold coins down his throat. This done, he appointed Nasrudin as the new governor.

One year passed, and word reached the palace that the new governor was also fiddling the books. Furious, the Shah-in-Shah resolved to punish Nasrudin in person. But when he arrived at the local treasury, he found all the money was made of spun sugar.

'What is the meaning of this outrage?!'

'If I am to receive the same punishment as my predecessor,' replied Nasrudin, 'I would prefer to enjoy the experience.'

Superlatives

Visitors to Tamerlane's Court were forever complaining about local rulers who demanded money and produce as a form of taxation. Tired of hearing their protests, Tamerlane instructed Nasrudin, who was serving as his aide, to compile a list of the greediest governors.

When Nasrudin presented the potentate with his findings some weeks later, Tamerlane was amazed to see his own name at the top of the list of offenders.

'Are you insane enough to think that I won't have you executed for your gall?' he asked.

'Your Majesty,' said Nasrudin, 'the majority of the men on the list are small-time criminals. They may be robbing their people blind, but you are the leader of the whole world. Had I placed a lesser man's name above yours, you — the greatest ruler of our time — would have appeared as second best.'

S

Sweet Revenge

Nasrudin sent his wife to borrow some sugar from their neighbours. When they sat down to eat the cake she had made, it tasted terrible. Meaning to play a joke on them, the neighbour had provided salt rather than sugar.

Vowing to get even, Nasrudin went into the chicken coop and gathered some droppings. These he ground and placed in a small snuff box. He then put a similar snuff box in his other pocket and left the house. He waited until he saw his neighbour and then took a pinch of real snuff from one box.

'Could I have a little of that?' asked the neighbour.

'You, my friend, must have the very best!' declared the Mulla, handing him the other box. The neighbour took a large pinch and sniffed.

'What is this revolting stuff?!' he choked.

'I believe my wife bought it where you buy your sugar,' replied the Mulla.

Swollen Feet

One day, Nasrudin was on the way to market when he saw his landlord coming down the path in the opposite direction. Owing the man several weeks rent, Nasrudin hid in a bush. But, as the landlord passed, he noticed a pair of feet sticking out from the shrubbery.

'Who is there?' he demanded.

'Just a little sparrow,' squeaked the Mulla.

'Nonsense, no sparrow has such large feet!'

'They used to be quite small,' replied the Mulla, 'but they have swollen due to the warm weather.'

S

Sympathy Pains

'Where were you yesterday?' demanded Nasrudin's enraged teacher, the day after the pupil had skipped school.

'My brother had a terrible toothache.'

'But you did not.'

'Nevertheless, I was needed at home.'

'Why?'

'To help with the moaning.'

S

Talking in Gestures

A famous Indian sage visited the Caliph of Baghdad's Court and asked to discuss certain theological matters with the palace's greatest religious leaders. However, the Muslim scholars were afraid that the visitor would get the better of them in argument. Instead of conversing with the sage, they elected Nasrudin to be their spokesman, secretly hoping that he would disgrace himself and be banished from the Court.

Since the two men did not share a common language, it was decided that they should communicate in mime.

The sage stepped forward and drew a circle in the centre of the room, then waited for Nasrudin's reply. The Mulla strode to the circle and divided it in two. Then he drew another line, thus sectioning it into four. He pointed to three of the segments and then to himself, and seemed to push the remaining quarter away.

The visitor appeared to understand this, and clasped his hands. He then started to open his palms and flutter his fingers up and down. Nasrudin answered by pointing to the circle. Again, the sage seemed to understand. He began to pat his stomach. Nasrudin responded by removing a boiled egg from his pocket, and made fluttering movements with his hand. The sage approached him and respectfully kissed his hand.

T

The courtiers were discomfited by the silent conversation, but the Caliph rewarded Nasrudin with his weight in gold.

Later, when Nasrudin had gone home, the Caliph started to wonder what the conversation was about. Employing a translator, he asked the Indian sage.

'For a long time,' replied the sage through the translator, 'Greek and Indian wise men have argued about the shape and origin of the world. Hoping to find out what Muslim thinkers had to say, I drew a circle on the ground to represent the globe. Your man firstly agreed that the Earth is indeed a sphere, then he divided it into two halves to signify north and south. He then divided the circle again, and offered one to me and kept three for himself. This I took to mean that three quarters of the world is sea, while the fourth is land. I decided to ask him about the vegetable world, and did this by fluttering my hands, meaning: "All that the world contains is born and exists thanks to the sun's rays and the rain from Heaven." Then I pointed to myself, hoping to explain about the multiplication of animals. Unfortunately, the sense of this last remark seemed to escape him and he took an egg from his pocket and flapped his hands, thus recalling the birds.

'In all, I am most impressed by the wisdom of your sage, and pleased that you have rewarded such a knowledgeable man.'

The Caliph was delighted, and summoned Nasrudin to give his version of events.

'Your guest was a greedy man with quite an appetite,' began the Mulla. 'First, he drew a circle on the ground which I took to signify a large plate of pulao. I drew a line across the plate to suggest that we might share the food, but he just stood there, in silence. His greed made me so angry that I split the plate again and offered him only a quarter of the pulao. Then I watched, amazed by his gluttony, as he raised his hands, meaning: "I wish they would bring stew!" I then attempted to point out, with gestures, that for stew you not only need meat, but vegetables and spices too. He just stood there and patted his stomach to stress his hunger. I then flapped my hands to tell him that I, too, was as light as a bird with hunger. I even showed him the boiled egg that I had hastily put in my pocket this morning because I had not had the time for breakfast. And that is the whole story!'

T

Tamerlane's Death

'If you are a true mystic,' Tamerlane said to Nasrudin, 'your powers will enable you to name the exact date of my death.'

Aware that the Emperor made a practice of rewarding the bearers of bad news with the gallows, Nasrudin replied:

'I do have details relevant to the day you will die, but before I divulge these I must have your word that whatever these details are, I will not feel your anger.'

'You have it!'

'You will die on a day of public celebration, O Zenith of Power! There will be dancing in the streets and feasting in every town and village of the Empire.'

'How can you be so sure, Sage?'

'Because on the day that you are taken ill, the people will rejoice and the celebrations will continue for the rest of your life and beyond.'

T

Teaching by Example

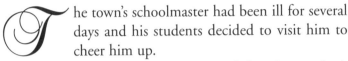

he town's schoolmaster had been ill for several days and his students decided to visit him to cheer him up.

The first schoolboy was surprised by the teacher's haggard appearance. 'Teacher! You have become as emaciated as a stray dog!' he cried.

The second pupil, a lad of far greater sensitivity, attempted to reassure the master. 'Don't worry about your lost strength. Soon your health will be restored. Your appetite will return. In no time at all you will once again be as fat as a pig.'

The teacher was most offended. In his weakened state, he complained to Nasrudin, his third visitor.

'What are things coming to? First I am called a dog, then a pig.'

'Please try not to upset yourself, master,' Nasrudin consoled. 'Remember, we three are only students. You are our teacher. And as is the teacher, so are the pupils.'

T

Terrible Nature

Nasrudin took his goose to market in order to sell it. An interested customer wanted to look at the bird, but it hissed at him and he hurried on his way. Another tried to feel its weight, but the goose pecked his hand sharply. A third, having seen the fate of the other two, observed:

'Your goose has a terrible nature.'

'Why do you think I am selling it?' replied Nasrudin.

T

The Angry Pot

Nasrudin was hurriedly attempting to cook a stew before his guests arrived. Grabbing a pot from the shelf, he dropped it on his foot. While he hopped about in pain, he lost his balance and cracked his elbow on the basin. Stumbling away, rubbing his elbow, he upset a pan of boiling water which scalded his hand. As he lay battered and burnt, he turned to the pot.

'You win! I will never handle you roughly again.'

T

The Best Liar

His Imperial Majesty the Shah-in-Shah had tired of his usual pastimes. He held up an enormous jewel-encrusted goblet and announced: 'Whoever can tell the most outrageous lie will receive this trophy as his reward.'

At once the Court Imam, a man of extremely wide girth and resplendent costume, rose to his feet.

'Your Majesty! I cannot allow this contest to proceed. Never has a lie passed my lips, as I know that untruth is a wicked and loathsome vice much deplored by God.'

The King simply laughed and turned to Nasrudin. 'Mulla, we all know what a fraud you are, why don't you begin?'

'Majesty, how delighted I would be to win such a glittering prize, but unfortunately there is no contest.'

'Explain yourself?'

'How can I hope to compete with the Imam? Surely he has offered a far more blatant lie than an amateur such as myself could come up with.'

The Best Teacher

The judge, Nasrudin's employer, sent him to find him a vicious guard dog.

After several hours, Nasrudin returned with a docile puppy.

'I told you to bring me a blood-thirsty monster of a dog!' the judge snarled.

'I know, Master, but the animal is still young enough to learn. And who could be a better teacher than yourself?'

T

The Beautiful Guest

*N*asrudin's wife had a young and attractive friend who came to stay. One night, during the visit, Nasrudin dreamt that the beautiful guest asked him to marry her. Waking up to find he had been dreaming, he shook his wife awake.

'Have nothing more to do with your friend,' he warned the sleepy woman. 'She is trying to steal me away from you.'

The Boastful King

---

*T*he King was an extremely arrogant man. One day, he was walking with Nasrudin in the palace gardens.

'I am the most cunning man in the land!' he boasted. 'There is none to match my wit. No one is able to outsmart one as shrewd as I.'

'It is true, Sire,' agreed Nasrudin. 'In fact, I can only think of one mortal more cunning than yourself.'

'More cunning? Impossible! Show me this man and I will soon make him look a fool.'

'He is waiting at the palace gates,' replied the Mulla. 'Wait right there and I will run and fetch him at once!'

A few minutes passed and the King grew impatient. 'Guards!' he growled, 'where is Nasrudin? I am waiting to meet a man who dares to think that he can outsmart me.'

'You have already met him,' muttered one of the servants.

T

The Butcher's Cat

Nasrudin's wife sent him to the bazaar to buy some meat on credit. The butcher refused to give him any meat unless he paid at once. Much offended, Nasrudin stormed out of the shop and, seeing the man's cat, stole it and took it home.

'I can't cook a cat!' exclaimed his appalled wife when she saw the animal.

'You will not have to,' replied the Mulla. Minutes later, there was a loud knock on the door.

'Give me my cat!' shouted the butcher. 'It is no use trying to deny that you stole it. My wife saw you.'

'Last night your cat crept into my store-room and ate two pounds of meat,' replied Nasrudin. 'The only way I can get the cat to return what is rightfully mine is to eat the useless creature, meat and all.'

The horrified butcher agreed to give Nasrudin two pounds of meat on the cat's behalf.

T

The Charmer

A wealthy businessman appeared before Judge Nasrudin on a fraud charge. Due to his reputation as a salesman, he was known as 'The Charmer'.

'Last night,' he told Nasrudin, 'I had a dream in which I went to Heaven and heard the angels in conversation. Allah had told them of the wisest of all sages. Think how my heart soared when I heard that this great man was you!'

'In other words,' said Nasrudin, 'this means that God will soon be enlisting my help in a legal case.'

T

The Cost of a Curse

Nasrudin was leaving the teahouse when he hit his head on the low door jamb and shouted: 'Damn you!'

Thinking the curse was directed at him, the proprietor took Nasrudin to court. Having listened to the plaintiff, the judge told Nasrudin to pay a shilling. The Mulla, forced to hand over his money, gave the judge a two-shilling piece.

While the court officials were hunting for the Mulla's change, he asked the judge:

'How much is the fine for cursing, again?'

'One shilling.'

'Then keep the change, damn you.'

The Cursed Leg

asrudin lent his favourite walking stick to his neighbour. When the man came to return the staff, the Mulla was dismayed to find it broken. 'How could you have destroyed it? That staff was like a left leg to me. Get away with you and may Allah repay you by depriving you of your own left leg!'

The neighbour, unimpressed by the Mulla's curse, started to walk away. He hadn't gone more than a few paces when he tripped on a tree stump and fell with his right leg twisted beneath him.

'How foolish I was to doubt your words!' he moaned, clutching his badly sprained ankle, 'But how is it that you cursed my left leg and my right leg was injured?'

'Your right leg is suffering in return for another man's staff you once borrowed and destroyed. You have yet to feel the consequences of my curse.'

T

The Desert Speaks

The King was told that Nasrudin could understand the language of inanimate objects. Intrigued, he told the Mulla to remain at his side until his powers could be put to the test.

A few days later, the royal convoy was working its way across the desert, when sand from one of the dunes rustled across their path.

'Nasrudin, tell us what the desert is trying to say.'

'It says: "Let the King remain on the throne and soon the whole country will be mine!"' replied the Mulla.

T

The Devil's Advice

Nasrudin was once delivering the sermon after prayers.

'As you are all aware, Allah made Adam out of clay and created Eve to keep him company. In Heaven, there also lived a demon called Azrail. Much attracted by Eve, he constantly pestered her in an indecent and lecherous way. This outrageous behaviour caused Allah to become very angry and he turned the demon into the Devil and cast him out of Paradise. Ever since, Satan has despised humans and tries, whenever possible, to trick them into sin.'

'What a coincidence that you have chosen today to speak of the Devil,' said one member of the congregation. 'For he came to me in a dream last night and told me that a man of my position, with two vast houses, should think twice before taking the word of an impoverished man living in a flimsy shack.'

'That is very interesting,' agreed Nasrudin. 'And did Satan, in this dream, suggest you give one of your dwellings to me?'

The Drowned Man Returns

Nasrudin was riding with his wealthy employer when that notable decided to swim in the river. Instructing the Mulla to stay on watch, he undressed and waded into the cool water. When he returned, much refreshed by his swim, he was surprised to see Nasrudin rush to meet him.

'Thanks be to Allah that you are not drowned!'

'And why should I be? The water is only a few feet deep.'

'When you were gone, I started worrying about your safety, and when you did not reappear for several minutes, I dispatched a horseman to carry the news of your death to your family. When I saw you emerge from the water, I sent a second messenger to stop the first. But unfortunately both men demanded payment.'

'And where did you find the money for these services?'

'In my panic, I took it from your purse.'

'And how is it that my purse, which had four gold coins in it, is now empty?'

'I had to pay each messenger one piece of gold, I paid a third coin as a deposit for your headstone, and the fourth I used to buy a kebab to steady my stomach, which had become upset by the chaotic events.'

T

The Forgotten Groom

Nasrudin was getting married, but the wedding guests were so excited by the event that they forgot to serve the bridegroom at the reception. Much offended, Nasrudin sat in a corner while all around him tucked into plates piled with savouries. After the meal, the guests called for the bridegroom:

'It is time to leave for your honeymoon!' they chorused, having found Nasrudin in his corner.

'Let those who ate my pulao go in my place,' said Nasrudin petulantly.

The Historian's Bet

'Nasrudin,' said the local historian, 'you always claim to know everything. I will give you ten gold pieces if you can tell me who was the mother of King Alexander.'

'Then you have lost your money,' replied the Mulla. 'She was the Queen.'

The Importance of Gold

'Nasrudin,' asked his miserly uncle, 'do you like gold?'

'Yes,' replied the Mulla, 'because a man who has gold does not have to ask favours of a scrooge like you.'

T

The Instructions Must be Followed

Nasrudin was penniless. After racking his brain for ways to make some money, he took a few pebbles and crushed them into powder. He then divided the powder into small piles. He wrapped each pile in some paper and set up a stall selling rat poison. Soon he was doing a roaring trade, with customers queuing to buy the powder. But the next day several returned, demanding a refund.

'You are a crook! We put your poison down and our houses are still crawling with vermin!' they ranted.

'Hang on a minute,' replied Nasrudin. 'Are you telling me that you scattered the powder and hoped to kill the rats?'

'Of course, what else does one do with poison?'

'What you should have done is grabbed a rat, struck its head on a hard surface, then opened its mouth and forced the powder down its throat. Do this and the poison is sure to work. Don't blame me if you fail to follow the instructions.'

The Keeper of the Shrine

he keeper of a much-visited shrine was always complaining.

'I never get a moment's peace. There is always a steady stream of pilgrims. Few ever make a donation and many ask for spiritual guidance, which bores me to tears. But what can be done?'

'Simple,' replied Nasrudin. 'Just tell them exactly what you have told me. Word will spread that you are a greedy and ignorant man, and the devotees will soon stop coming altogether.'

The King's Father

The King interviewed one hundred candidates for the post of Court astrologer. He told each to read his destiny in the stars.

'You will be the greatest ruler the world has ever known!' sang one.

'You will live a hundred years,' chanted another. Each man struggled to give a more favourable reading than the last. Finally, it was Nasrudin's turn to impress the monarch.

'Your children and wife are in good health. And your father will live until he is ninety,' said the Mulla.

'That is impossible!' snorted the King. 'My father died years ago at the age of fifty-seven.'

'The stars never lie,' insisted Nasrudin.

'How dare you argue?' raged the King. 'I will have you imprisoned for your impertinence!'

'But, Your Majesty,' replied Nasrudin, 'how can you be absolutely sure of the identity of your real father?'

Nasrudin was released and appointed Court astrologer.

T

The King's Horse

While Nasrudin was the King's equerry, his master came to inspect the stables. 'Is my charger worthy of the King?' he asked the Mulla.

'No, Your Majesty.'

'Is the beast fit for the Greatest Warrior the World Has Ever Seen to ride into battle?'

'No, Your Majesty.'

'Is it a just mount for the Ruler of the Universe?'

'No, Your Majesty.'

'Then tell me, man, what is it good for?'

'For me to saddle up and ride away,' replied the equerry, 'so that I may escape your ridiculous boasts.'

The King's Messengers

While Nasrudin was a Court messenger, he was dispatched to the house of a local governor. Seeing the Mulla's ragged coat and unkempt beard, the arrogant governor wrinkled his nose.

'What message do you bring?'

'One from the King himself!' trumpeted Nasrudin. 'He wishes you to attend a banquet at the palace tonight.'

'I will gladly accept the invitation, if only to comment in person on the poor appearance of the King's messenger. Are there no presentable men to carry the King's invitations?'

'Yes, many, but they have been sent to the many dignitaries more important than yourself.'

T

The King's Scraps

When Nasrudin left Tamerlane's Court to plough his fields, the Ruler of the World soon started to miss the Mulla's jokes. One day, when he had finished eating, he had his servants clear the remains of the feast from the table and take them to Nasrudin with a message that he should return to Court.

The twenty servants, each bearing a platter piled high with delicacies, duly arrived at the Mulla's humble dwelling.

'The Ruler of the Universe has ordered us to bring you and your family food from his own table, and demands you to return to amuse him as soon as you have eaten your fill,' the head servant announced.

The rich aromas of the food caused Nasrudin's mouth to water, but, instead of inviting the servants in he said haughtily:

'Go to the field at the back of the house and offer the food to my goats. But, please, do not tell them that these are left-overs, for they are proud creatures and may refuse the food.'

T

The King's Shadow

*T*he King was extremely superstitious. He sought advice from various fortune-tellers and astrologers. One day, he asked Nasrudin to interpret his latest dream.

'I had the most terrifying nightmare that I turned into the Devil himself.'

'Very interesting,' replied the Mulla, 'and what did the Devil look like?'

'It is hard to say, but I suppose he looked most like a donkey.'

'Do not be afraid, Your Highness,' said Nasrudin. 'You were not frightened by Satan in your dream, but by your own shadow.'

The King's Tail

Nasrudin's family was so poor that they had no money for food.

One day, when the cupboard was completely bare, the Mulla went to ask the King for a loan. As is often the case with rich men, the monarch was in a bad mood and had his guards throw the Mulla into the street. Empty-handed, Nasrudin returned home.

Next day, the King regretted his bad behaviour towards Nasrudin, who was something of a Court favourite. He called for his stallion and rode to the Mulla's house. As he approached the dwelling, he was surprised to hear the sounds of feasting. He hastily returned to the palace to check that no funds were missing from the royal coffers.

Satisfied that nothing was missing, he summoned Nasrudin to explain his new-found wealth.

'Yesterday, you came to me cap in hand, whining that your family was starving. How is it that, today, you have the money to throw a banquet?'

'I have made a few choice wagers, Majesty,' replied the Mulla.

The King asked him to explain further, but he would say no more.

'If you wish, Your Majesty, you may also join me in a bet. I am willing to wager a hundred gold pieces that come tomorrow morning, you will have grown a bushy tail.' Thinking that the Mulla had finally taken leave of his

T

senses, the King readily agreed to the bet.

All that night he tossed and turned, fearing that through some sorcery he might grow a tail. But, come morning, he was still tailless and hurried off to collect his gold.

'Nasrudin!' he crowed, 'you have lost, so hand over my money.'

'First, we must check that you have no tail,' replied the Mulla, escorting the King into the guest room. Still chuckling the King removed his trousers. There was not even the merest hint of a tail, and Nasrudin handed him a purse of gold and the King took his leave.

Later that day a messenger, wearing a resplendent uniform and riding a well-proportioned dapple grey, arrived at the palace with an invitation from Nasrudin to the King. The Mulla was throwing another banquet and humbly requested the pleasure of the Monarch's company.

Intrigued, the King accepted and arrived at Nasrudin's house at the appointed time.

As he was being ushered into the house, he whispered to his host: 'I must ask you something. Yesterday, you threw a party; this morning you gave me one hundred pieces of gold. Where is all this money coming from?'

'Majesty,' replied the Mulla, 'as I told you some days ago, I made a few wagers. I bet ten of the wealthiest men in town that I would be able to get the King to remove his trousers in front of a crowd. This morning, you did just that. For those ten men were watching under the window. At one hundred pieces of gold each, I have made one thousand pieces of gold. More than enough to pay my lost bet to you and celebrate in style!'

T

The King's Voice

*T*he King fancied himself as a great singer. One day, he summoned Nasrudin and told him to listen to his latest song. After the first few notes, Nasrudin burst into laughter.

'What a terrible voice!' he chuckled with tears rolling down his face. Much aggrieved, the King had the Mulla locked away in the dungeon for two weeks. At the end of that time, he summoned Nasrudin once again.

'I have another song for you, Sage. Perhaps your time in a cell has attuned your ear.'

When the King was halfway through the song, he saw Nasrudin leaving the room and stopped.

'Where do you think you are going?'

'Back to my cell.'

T

The King's Worth

'Nasrudin,' asked the King, 'you are Court treasurer. Tell me, how much is your Sovereign worth?'

'A hundred gold pieces, Sire.'

'How dare you name such a paltry amount! My sword alone is worth that!'

'Indeed, Your Majesty, I have estimated your value on your sword, without which you would not be my Sovereign.'

The Letter

'Nasrudin, could you write a letter to my cousin in Samarkand?' asked an illiterate. 'He has gone on a trip and I want to know when he will be back.'

'My handwriting is so bad that he may have trouble reading the letter, but I will certainly write it.' said the Mulla. 'If he cannot decipher any of the words, ask him to bring it to me.'

T

The Mayor's an Ass

On his way back from market, Nasrudin stopped to rest. Lulled by the sound of a nearby brook he fell deeply asleep. When he finally awoke, he found that his donkey had run off.

'If you're looking for your ass,' said a practical joker, 'it has been appointed mayor of the neighbouring town.' Thanking the man, Nasrudin hurried to the next town. Sure enough, there was a new mayor — a man with an unusually thick grey beard and prominent ears.

'Let me be among the first to congratulate you on your appointment,' said the Mulla.

'Thank you very much,' replied the dignitary. 'Did you vote for me?'

'Hah!' quipped Nasrudin. 'As if I'd waste my vote on a donkey!'

Deciding that Nasrudin must be an escaped madman, the mayor attempted to make small talk until reinforcements arrived.

'You'll see, my friend. I have great plans to rebuild this town.'

'An ass that plans to rebuild!' whooped Nasrudin, mopping tears from his eyes. 'Before you get too busy, do one last thing for me. Carry this sack of rice to my house on your back.'

At this insulting behaviour, the mayor's good humour faded. He ordered that Nasrudin be run out of town. Fleeing from the mob, who were baying for his blood, the Mulla sprinted home. Outside the house with head held low, he found the donkey.

'Aha!' he crowed, 'you have finally realised that you are not cut out for the onerous duties of mayor!'

T

The Miserly Cave

Nasrudin once journeyed through the Himalayas. Slipping and sliding on the thick snow, he came to a cave, in the mouth of which hung an array of enormous icicles. Never having seen these before, he mistook them for crystals and hurriedly broke some off and hid them away in his saddle-bag. He then built a camp-fire and lay down to rest. Just before he continued on his way, he couldn't resist taking another look at his new treasures. But when he opened his bag, he found that the crystals had vanished. Not realising that they had melted in the heat, he turned frowning to the cave:

'I had no idea that you were so miserly!' he exclaimed. 'If material things mean so much to you, then have these and choke on them!' And he threw his saddle-bags into the cave's mouth.

T

The Missing Tail

Nasrudin needed money and had nothing left to sell but his donkey. With a heavy heart, he groomed the animal and prepared to set off for the donkey bazaar. Leaving the stable, he realised it was raining, so he cut off the donkey's tail to stop it getting muddy. He then stuffed the tail in his bag. At the bazaar, several buyers approached him, but seeing that the tail was missing, they lost interest.

Towards the end of the day, a potential customer came by and offered the Mulla two gold pieces for the donkey, which he accepted after much haggling. It was only when the new owner started to lead the animal away that he noticed that it had no tail.

'Give me back my money, there is nothing less attractive that an incomplete beast.'

'But the donkey is complete.'

'How can you say that? It has no tail.'

'Oh! I almost forgot,' said the Mulla, handing the man the donkey's tail.

T

The Most Tolerant Man

Nasrudin was dining with some of the village elite. Soon conversation turned to the merits of generosity and tolerance.

'I am surely the most generous and tolerant man here!' rasped the judge. 'Think how rarely I impose the death penalty.'

'I am far more tolerant,' claimed the mayor. 'Think of all the taxes I do not take.'

'Actually,' said the Imam, 'I am the most generous and tolerant man in the village. Think of all the men who deserve to die for their lack of religious understanding, but I merely have them flogged.'

'You are all wrong,' replied Nasrudin, 'I am the tolerant, generous and patient one. When you three divided up my share of the food tonight, I sat here and said nothing.'

The New House

Nasrudin was being shown over his father-in-law's new mansion. Trekking from room to room, the Mulla soon worked up a considerable appetite, but no mention of food was made by his host.

Finally, the two men came to the kitchen, and Nasrudin lingered in the room for a while.

'I see that you are suitably impressed by the kitchen, too,' grunted his father-in-law.

'Yes,' replied Nasrudin, 'it is such a well-equipped room that no man could enter it without his stomach crying for food.'

T

The Only Cure

While Nasrudin was a doctor, a practical joker came to see him.

'Last night I coughed for hours.'

'Had you caught a chill?'

'No, I slept with my mouth open and inadvertently swallowed a spider.'

'Then there is only one cure; you will have to swallow a cat.'

T

Theoretical Knowledge

Nasrudin was keen to offer his two sons a decent education. With this in mind, he sent them away to be educated at the country's highest seat of learning.

When, years later, the sons returned as fully-fledged philosophers, he decided to test their skills.

'Take this saddle and place it on my donkey,' he said to the academics. Instead of carrying out the simple task, the philosophers sat down and started to discuss the problem from all angles. By dusk, they had still not managed to reach a decision.

'Just as I thought!' said their dispirited father. 'All this theoretical knowledge makes you about as intelligent as the donkey itself!'

T

The Other Five

he judge was unable to decide which of six men had stolen the Imam's turban, so he sentenced all six to jail.

'We are innocent,' insisted five of them, 'Please release us!'

'I did it,' admitted the sixth. 'And I am glad!'

'You had better release the guilty man,' advised Nasrudin, 'or he will corrupt the other five.'

T

The Plague

Tamerlane was always boasting that his Empire had never been struck by an epidemic during his reign. Then, one day, word reached the palace that plague had broken out in Samarkand. The Ruler of the World immediately gave the order for his servants to prepare his luggage.

'Do not leave us!' wept the courtiers, throwing themselves at the Emperor's feet.

Nasrudin was the only person to smile:

'What a pity that the plague took so long to reach the city.'

T

The Poorer Man

One day, Tamerlane and Nasrudin were walking through the town. When the Emperor passed a beggar on the street, he asked the man's name.

'When I was born, my parents called me "Riches",' the man replied.

'How amusing that you turned out to be so poor!' cackled the ruler.

'It is obvious which of you two is the poorer,' said Nasrudin. 'The one who laughs at the misfortune of the other.'

T

The Price of Mercy

When his donkey died, Nasrudin was so devastated that he refused to eat. 'Why are you determined to starve to death?' asked his wife. 'Allah gave you one donkey. Surely He will show mercy and give you another.'

'That is what I am afraid of,' replied Nasrudin. 'The last time He showed mercy and gave me a donkey, it cost ten gold coins. Who knows how expensive His mercy will be next time?'

T

The Same Reason

When Nasrudin's first wife died, he married a widow. But she was always crying when she remembered her late husband. One day, when she burst into tears for the third time in an hour, she was surprised to see that Nasrudin was crying, too.

'I am crying because my poor husband is dead,' she blubbered. 'But why are you crying?'

'For the same reason. For if he had not died, I would not be married to you.'

T

The Servant's Footsteps

One day, the town governor hired Nasrudin to find his missing cook. As the Mulla searched, he whistled a merry tune.

'Why are you whistling?' asked a man on the road.

'Because I am looking for the governor's cook, who has gone missing.'

'But why should that make you so happy?'

'Because I'm hoping that for once the master will follow in the servant's footsteps,' replied Nasrudin.

T

The Sky is Falling

asrudin was sitting under an apple tree. 'Almighty Allah,' he prayed, 'send your servant a piece of gold so that he can buy bread.' At that moment an apple fell from the tree and hit Nasrudin on the top of the head.

'God is so angry that I have asked for money that He is throwing pieces of the sky at me!' yelped the Mulla.

Later, as he was walking through the bazaar, he heard a preacher, surrounded by a crowd, crying: 'O Allah, send me not ten, not twenty, but a hundred gold pieces!'

'You fool!' shouted the Mulla. 'Are you trying to send the whole universe crashing down on our heads?'

The Storm

Nasrudin was sitting with some friends in the teahouse.

'Did you hear the terrible storm last night?' one asked the other.

'Yes! Never have I heard such blood-curdling thunder. I almost jumped out of my skin,' replied the second man, and asked Nasrudin what he had thought of the storm.

'Was there really a storm last night?"

'Didn't you hear it for yourself?'

'No, but I am not surprised. My mother-in-law visited last night and I suppose the storm broke while she was talking to my wife.'

T

The Stronger Oath

One day, the Imam accused Nasrudin of being a fraud:

'I am willing to swear on the Prophet that not a single one of your mystic observations is true!'

'And I swear by Adam that all I have said is true!' replied the Mulla.

A crowd of onlookers, choosing to believe the Imam rather than the Mulla, grabbed Nasrudin and took him to the King.

'I am told that you are a fraud,' the King said to the Mulla. 'If I find that you are also a blasphemer, you will suffer the most horrible of punishments.'

'Everyone has taken leave of their senses!' snapped Nasrudin. 'How can I be guilty when my oath was the stronger of the two. The Prophet was a man, but Adam was the ancestor of all men, and for this reason my oath renders any oath involving one of his descendants null and void.'

T

The Sun's Game

Nasrudin settled down for a nap under a tree. As the sun moved round, the shade moved and he felt his skin beginning to burn. With a sigh, he shuffled back into the shade and dozed off. Half an hour later, the sun was burning him again. Muttering, he again changed places. Soon, he felt the sun's rays on his skin once more. Jumping to his feet he looked up at the sun:

'You may find this amusing now, but just wait until you are trying to sleep. I'll come and bother you!'

T

The Swimming Bucket

*N*asrudin went to the well to draw some water. As he lowered the rope it snapped, and the bucket fell to the bottom with a loud splash. With a sigh, the Mulla sat down on the wall of the well.

'Are you sunning yourself, Mulla?' asked a friend who happened to pass by some minutes later.

'No, I'm waiting for my bucket. It dived into the well for a swim and now seems reluctant to leave the cool water.'

T

The Thrifty Imam

Nasrudin and a few friends were invited to the Imam's house for supper. Their host was renowned for his meanness. Before the meal, he delivered a three-hour sermon on the merits of thrift.

The guests, fading away from hunger, were much relieved when the Imam signalled his servants to bring the first course. A huge tureen of vegetable soup was placed on the table. The Imam took a spoon and tasted the aromatic liquid.

'Take this away at once! It is far too salty!'

The guests watched, speechless, as the tureen was removed. Next, roast mutton was brought. Again, the Imam took a bite and waved the plate away, ordering it to be taken back to the kitchen. 'Are you trying to kill us all?' he shrieked to the cook. 'This meat is rotting away.'

Finally, two platters piled high with pulao were brought. The Imam lifted his spoon to sample the rice. Before he had time to lift the food to his lips, Nasrudin seized the platter and heaped the pulao on his and the other guests' plates.

'While our respected host continues to train his new cook, let us fill in time by eating.'

T

The Ugly Emperor

*T*amerlane was so impressed by the traveller Nasrudin, that he asked him to stay at Court indefinitely. One night, the Mulla entered the throne room and found the King in tears.

'Forgive me for asking, Majesty, but why do you weep?'

'For the first time in twenty-five years I have looked in the mirror, and I was devastated to find that the Ruler of the World, the Mightiest Conqueror, is ugly.'

'You have looked at yourself once in all these years,' replied Nasrudin wonderingly. 'Perhaps you now understand why your subjects sob as you walk by.'

T

The World's End

'Nasrudin,' asked his wife, 'what day of the week will the end of the world come?' 'Whichever day of the week I die,' replied Nasrudin. 'For that will be the day on which your relatives and my relatives start to squabble over my possessions.'

T

The Worn Coin

*N*asrudin decided to have a massage at the public baths. The masseur was so rough that, afterwards, the Mulla felt as if he had been thrown by his donkey and trampled beneath its hooves.

Handing the man a coin so worn that it was just a sliver of metal, he prepared to leave the bath house.

'Hey!' complained the masseur, 'this coin is almost worn away.'

'I know,' replied Nasrudin. 'My hands have worn it until it has almost disappeared, just as your hands have done to me.'

Thieves and Chickens

One dark night, thieves broke into Nasrudin's house. 'Do something or they will surely steal everything we own,' said Nasrudin's wife.

At that moment his chickens began to cluck in the garden.

'This is what we will do,' said one thief to the other as the couple listened upstairs. 'We will kill the chickens, roast them and eat them. Then we'll cut Nasrudin's throat and make off with his wife.'

Hearing this, Nasrudin began to whimper with fear. So eerie was the sound that the two thieves took fright and ran away.

'What sort of coward are you,' said his wife, 'that you whimper with fear during a break-in?'

'That's easy for you to say,' replied Nasrudin, 'but do you think the reason the thieves ran off matters to me or the chickens?'

T

Time to Doze

While Nasrudin was guard to a wealthy businessman, his master often found him asleep.

'If you have enough time to doze then you have enough time to work!' grated his master, and put Nasrudin in charge of the mansion's kitchens.

Several weeks later, he told Nasrudin to come and discuss the menu for a banquet he was to hold. As the Mulla waddled into the room, his master was surprised by how fat he had become.

'How your waist has widened. Soon you will not fit through the door!'

'It is not the door that I worry about, but I would like a wider bed.'

T

To Fool the Cat

One day, Nasrudin returned from the bazaar with a chicken in a sack.

'What have you there?' asked his wife.

'Just some carrots,' replied the Mulla. His wife took the sack and put it in the kitchen. That night, the cat sniffed at the bag, and ate the chicken.

'Wife!' shouted the Mulla, next morning, 'what have you done with the meat?'

'What meat?'

'The chicken I brought home yesterday.'

'You said the sack contained carrots, so I put it in the kitchen.'

'Stupid woman!' exclaimed Nasrudin, 'I only said that to fool the cat!'

Tongue on the Loose

Nasrudin was travelling in India when he met another traveller on the road. 'Where have you come from?' enquired the man.

'From Bombay,' replied the Mulla.

'And where are you going?'

'To Delhi,' came the reply.

'What have you thought of those you have met on your travels?'

'In general, the common people have proved kind and hospitable,' said Nasrudin. 'I hear that the governor of Bombay is a tyrant indeed. It is said that he is a thousand times more oppressive than Genghis Khan himself!'

'And do you know who I am?' asked the stranger in a strained voice.

'I am afraid I am new around here, and have not had the honour…'

'I am the governor of whom you speak!'

'Alas, what a shame it is that we have met on a day when my tongue has decided to work without the use of my brain!' said Nasrudin sadly.

Tonics

Nasrudin was called out to heal a rich land-owner. 'Quick, give me a tonic to stop my stomach from splitting in two!'

'But what if the tonic fails to cure you?'

'How can it? You yourself once told me of its magic ingredients.'

'And what if I was mistaken?'

'Stop delaying. Without the medicine I will surely die.'

'With the medicine you will also die,' replied Doctor Nasrudin. 'It is just a matter of when and from what.'

T

Too Good for Promotion

*T*eenage Nasrudin went to work for the local blacksmith. After several months, the boy's father realised that he had never seen his son's handiwork. 'After all this time, you must soon be ready to set up on your own.'

'Not yet,' replied the teenager. 'So far, I have been minding the smith's children and cooking his meals, but he promises that as soon as I am no good at this work, my true apprenticeship will begin.'

Too Heavy a Load

asrudin spent the whole morning collecting rubbish from the town dump in the hope that he could sell it in the bazaar. Seeing the Mulla's donkey stumbling along with such a heavy load, an old man called out:

'Shame on you! That poor beast has far too much on his back!'

Nasrudin immediately removed the load and packed it onto his own back, then climbed into the saddle.

'Thank you for pointing it out. I had not realised how heavy these things were.'

Too Hot to Eat

One day, Nasrudin's mother gave him some pastries fresh from the oven. Stubbornly, the boy began to force each sizzling pie into his mouth. 'Listen, my child, those are your pies, nobody will take them away, so wait until they are cool enough to eat without pain.'

'If I do that,' said Nasrudin, mopping the tears from his eyes, 'I will still be hungry.'

T

Too Late

Nasrudin went to buy some nuts but, seeing the stall unattended, he started to consume as many nuts as possible in the merchant's absence. By the time the stallholder returned, Nasrudin had eaten his fill. Seeing the empty trays, the merchant realised what had happened and started to beat the Mulla.

'What a strange man you are!' declared Nasrudin. 'You didn't kick me when I wanted your nuts, but now I don't want them you beat me black and blue!'

T

Too Many Salesmen

*N*asrudin decided to become a travelling salesman. He loaded luxurious fabrics, spices, tin pots and other tempting items onto his donkey and set off for town.

'Silk from China!' he called, 'Saffron and paprika! Ribbons and baubles, buttons and buckles!' But every time he tried to publicise his wares, the donkey brayed so loudly that his words were drowned out.

No amount of hitting it or begging would silence the beast. Finally, he lost patience.

'Listen!' he said, turning to the ass, 'There is no room for two salesmen. Either you tell people about our wares and I will keep quiet, or I will tell them and you can keep quiet. When we both try at once, our voices clash and no one can make out the words.'

The donkey was silent, and Nasrudin continued on his way. But the second he opened his mouth, the beast started to bray louder than before.

'Very well!' howled the Mulla, 'You sell our goods and I will go home.' And dropping the reins, he strode off alone.

T

Trading at a Loss

'*I*'m sick of you sitting around and doing nothing all day,' complained Nasrudin's wife one day. 'If you don't find an occupation at once, I shall leave you.'

Nasrudin went straight to the bazaar where he bought some pies at a silver piece for ten. He then set up a stall next to the baker and began selling the pies at a silver piece for twenty.

'What are you playing at?' demanded the irate baker. 'You're taking all my business and trading at a loss.'

'What has business and loss got to do with all this?' replied Nasrudin, 'I'm just finding an occupation.'

T

Translations

While Nasrudin was in Baghdad, the powerful head of the Great Mosque attacked him as an infidel.

'You are just pretending to be a sage, but in fact, you are a non-believer and an ignoramus! I bet that you do not even understand Arabic, the language in which the Holy Book is written!'

'And if I understand a sentence you say in Arabic,' replied Nasrudin, 'will you accept that I am a better man than you?'

'Happily!' promised the spiritual leader, 'If you will accept a hundred lashes if you fail.'

'Happily,' replied Nasrudin.

The great man then said, in Arabic: 'You cannot make leather out of the hide of a dog.'

Nasrudin immediately translated the sentence: 'You cannot make leather out of the hide of the head of the Great Mosque.'

T

Troublesome Foot

Nasrudin was washing his feet before prayer when the water ran out and he was only able to cleanse one foot. He hopped into the mosque and stood on one leg as the Imam led the prayers. Afterwards, the cleric called Nasrudin over.

'What is the meaning of this? Why were you hopping about while at prayer?'

'Quite simple,' replied the Mulla. 'My left foot is forever causing trouble. Today it was so badly behaved that it did not wash. As punishment I decided not to let it pray.'

T

True Justice

*H*earing that Nasrudin was a man of considerable wisdom, an affluent land-owner arrived at his house to offer his respects. But when he saw the Mulla's ragged coat and modest dwelling, he lost all respect for his host.

'I have been told that you are a great thinker and a proponent of true justice. How can a man who lives in poverty be capable of any wisdom at all? Look at me, I have never had to do a day's work in my life and yet, through rent, I have amassed a fortune so great that I would not have enough hours in the day to count it.'

'When I find a master who sees the world as I do,' replied Nasrudin, 'I will be as rich as you.'

'Are you daring to suggest that His Majesty Tamerlane the Great is an unfit ruler?' demanded the nobleman.

'That depends on whom he rules,' responded his host. 'It is perfectly clear that he is a most suitable master for a parasite such as yourself.'

T

True Vision

While in the famous city of Samarkand, Nasrudin went to hear the teachings of the Imam of the principal mosque. In the middle of the most eloquent address, the great man suddenly roared:

'Get away, you mangy cur!' He then continued the sermon as if nothing had happened.

Afterwards, Nasrudin approached the Imam. 'That was surely the most uplifting lecture I have been honoured enough to hear,' he said, kissing the priest's hand. 'But dare I ask why you interrupted the speech halfway through?'

'Simple,' replied the Imam. 'So close am I to all things holy that I saw quite clearly the vision of a stray dog approaching the Kaaba in Mecca. Naturally, I took it upon myself to frighten the unclean animal away.'

Some months later, the same Imam passed by Nasrudin's small town. The Mulla quickly invited everyone he knew to dinner to mark the arrival of such a revered man.

When the food arrived, Nasrudin served his guests with chicken and rice, except for the Imam, to whom he served an enormous plate of lamb pulao. So as not to offend the other diners, he had hidden the meat under a layer of rice.

T

Presented with a dish of meatless pulao the affronted guest of honour refused the food.

'How extraordinary,' observed the Mulla. 'Our esteemed guest has the vision to see a dog approach the Kaaba, but cannot detect a layer of lamb hidden under rice!'

Trumpeters at Court

asrudin's neighbour was learning to play the trumpet. After many sleepless nights listening to the tortuous notes, Nasrudin could stand it no longer. He knocked on the man's door.

'I have come to tell you that the King is thinking of making you his second-in-command.'

Delighted, the neighbour asked Nasrudin for advice.

'Should I go to the palace straight away?'

'I suggest that you wait a while. Before making your appointment public, he has to find another role for the man who currently holds the position.'

The neighbour agreed to keep the news secret until he was called to the Court. A few days later, Nasrudin knocked on his door again.

'It is not good, my friend,' he said. 'Apparently the Court astrologer has warned that no trumpeter should hold a position close to the King.'

'Nasrudin,' wailed the neighbour, 'what shall I do?'

'I suppose that if you were to swear, before witnesses, that you would never play the trumpet again, you would cease to be a trumpeter,' he replied.

His neighbour found a Qur'an and two witnesses and vowed never to play the trumpet again.

Next day, Nasrudin knocked on his door for the third time. 'Bad news. The King has appointed his nephew to the post. What a shame you have lost a distinguished position at Court and cut short your musical career.'

T

Turning in his Grave

One day, a sage invited himself and various followers to dine at Nasrudin's house. As the guests greedily consumed the last morsels of food in the house, the sage said:

'Last night I dreamt of your father, a truly generous man. He was much worried by your destitution'

'Really?' asked the surprised Mulla. 'What else did he say?'

'He said that it was a great shame that such an honoured guest as I should be served with a mere bowl of soup.'

Nasrudin had no choice. He went out and bought a whole roast goat which he immediately placed before the wise man.

The next week, the sage returned at supper time with another gaggle of followers.

'I had to come, Nasrudin,' he said, 'to tell you that I have once again dreamt of your worthy father. This time, he said that he could not rest unless his son offered even greater hospitality to such an important man as myself.'

Without a word, Nasrudin rushed out and spent his last savings on a fat-tailed sheep. Again, he sat back and watched his guests devour every last scrap of the meal.

The third week, the sage arrived with a throng of

~412~

disciples all clamouring to be fed.

'Mulla,' intoned the wise man, 'your father has come to me in yet another dream.'

'Before you continue,' broke in the impoverished Nasrudin, 'I must point out that a man with such elevated thoughts as yourself is probably not aware that we have no oxen in this land. Otherwise you, my revered visitor, would certainly have asked your humble host to supply roast ox for supper.'

T

Two Coins Behind

Nasrudin owed a local tradesman money. One day, the man came into the teahouse where the Mulla was sitting with some friends.

'I am surprised that a man of your standing, Mulla, does not pay his debts.'

'How much do I owe you?'

'Twenty gold pieces.'

'And if I pay you six tomorrow?'

'Fourteen.'

'And six the next day?'

'Eight.'

'And six the day after?'

'Two.'

'I am surprised that a man of your standing troubles his customers when they fall only two coins behind.'

T

Two Disasters

asrudin was at the Emperor's palace in Samarkand when a messenger arrived bearing news of famine in an enemy land.

'Thanks be to Allah, famine has not reached my great empire since I have been on the throne,' boasted the Conqueror.

'Allah may move in mysterious ways,' said Nasrudin, 'but surely even He would not send two disasters to Samarkand at one time.'

Two Saddle-bags

Two traders appeared before the Court where Nasrudin was sitting as judge. They had recently returned from a trip to Baghdad where each had bought a sack of dried apricots and each had placed his share of the fruit in his beautiful saddle-bag. On the trip home, they had fed themselves on the apricots, but rather than eating their own stores, they had stolen each other's. By the time they reached home, both bags were empty.

When he had heard the story, Nasrudin gave each man the other's saddle-bag. 'You have now both been compensated for your loss,' he said, 'but before you leave, there is the matter of Court costs to consider.' And to cover these, the judge took both saddle-bags.

T

Two Shoes More

asrudin's donkey finally died of old age and the Mulla was forced to walk from place to place. One day, he was walking into town when he found a horseshoe on the path. He pocketed it and carried on his way. Some paces later he found another horseshoe.

He was delighted. 'At this rate, I will have a whole donkey by sunset!'

T

Two Tricksters

A practical joker, staying with Nasrudin, decided to make his host the butt of one of his pranks. That night he crept into the Mulla's room and painted a wide grin on his face. The Mulla, who was only feigning sleep, let the trickster have his fun. Two hours later, when the other man was asleep, he stole into his room and shaved the back of his head.

Next morning, host and guest sat at the breakfast table.

'Tell me Nasrudin,' giggled the joker, 'why do you grin so?'

'I grin to see the ridiculous haircut you have chosen,' replied Nasrudin.

T

Two Wood-cutters

One day, two wood-cutters came to see the judge. 'We have just returned from selling our wood at the bazaar,' said one, 'and my colleague here says he is entitled to half our profits.'

'Is that not fair?' asked the judge.

'It would be if he had done an honest day's work,' replied the man, 'but while I took my axe, he sat on a stump and did nothing.'

'That is not true,' said the other. 'While you swung your axe, I shouted "thwack" to encourage you.'

'He may have shouted "thwack" but I did all the hard work!' said the first.

'But you wouldn't have been able to keep it up without my encouragement,' said the second.

Having heard the evidence, the judge pondered, but try as he might, he could not reach a verdict.

'May I intervene, Your Honour?' asked Nasrudin, after several minutes had elapsed. Given permission to do so, he took a coin and threw it into the air. It landed with a 'clink'.

'Did you hear that sound?' he asked the second wood-cutter.

'Yes,' replied the man.

'Then take that "clink" in payment for your "thwack" and leave the court,' said Nasrudin.

T

Unable to Help

Nasrudin and a friend bought the ingredients for stew.

'Mulla,' said the friend, 'you cut the vegetables while I prepare the meat.'

'Unfortunately, I haven't the slightest idea how the vegetables should be sliced,' replied Nasrudin.

'Then you prepare the meat and I will cut the vegetables.'

'Alas, I cannot,' replied the Mulla. 'Raw meat makes me feel ill.'

'Very well, go and light the stove. I will prepare the stew.'

'If only I could,' said Nasrudin, 'but sadly, I am afraid of fire.'

Losing patience, the friend did all the work himself. Soon he had cooked an aromatic stew. Nasrudin served himself a huge helping and started to eat the food with enormous appetite.

Seeing the Mulla spooning stew greedily into his mouth, his friend sarcastically remarked: 'I see that you are also unable to eat stew.'

'Alas, yes,' agreed Nasrudin, 'but I am trying my best because I know how much trouble you took to make it.'

U

Unhappy at Home

asrudin was listening to the Imam's sermon one day.

'The Prophet Mohammed was a great family man,' announced the Imam.

'It is all very well to be a great family man if you have angels on your side,' interrupted Nasrudin from the back of the mosque. 'If your wife gives you any trouble, you only have to call the Angel of Death to take her away.'

'Nasrudin,' said the Imam, 'are you saying that you are unhappy with your wife?'

'Isn't every man here?'

Deciding to put the Mulla's statement to the test, the Imam asked any man unhappy with his wife to raise his right hand.

Immediately, a forest of arms went up. Only Nasrudin remained still.

'Mulla, you are confused,' said the Imam. 'One minute you say you are unhappy with your wife, the next you are the only man not to raise his hand.'

'I am not leaving my hand at my side because I am happy,' said Nasrudin. 'I am keeping my hand down because I am incapable of raising it. This morning my wife threw a fire grate at me and broke my arm.'

U

Unorthodox Means

While Nasrudin was judge, three suspects in a burglary trial appeared before him. There were no eyewitnesses and no clear evidence to identify which of the three was guilty of the crime.

Handing each man a length of rope, Nasrudin ordered that they appear before him at the same time next day: 'Two of the lengths will remain the same, but the thief's rope will grow another ten inches by morning.'

That night, the two innocent men slept soundly, but the guilty man tossed and turned, plagued by his conscience. He eventually got out of bed and cut ten inches from his rope.

When the men presented themselves in court next day, the judge inspected their ropes. Two of the lengths had remained the same, the third was several inches shorter.

The thief was identified. 'You can't accuse me on such unorthodox evidence!' he clamoured, as Nasrudin prepared to pass sentence.

'Very well,' replied the judge. 'We will reach a verdict by orthodox means. Remove this man's shirt and we will get the rope to make him confess a second time.'

Hearing this, the man immediately confessed.

U

Useful Stones

One morning, Nasrudin was attacked by brigands on his way to the King's Court. He was robbed, beaten and left for dead by the roadside. Eventually he regained consciousness and managed to limp home. A few weeks later, the Mulla was again visiting the palace. On his way, he filled his pockets with stones. As the King addressed his courtiers, the stones fell noisily from Nasrudin's coat.

The monarch interrupted his speech:

'Nasrudin, do you not find that pockets full of stones are an unnecessary burden?'

'Majesty,' replied the Mulla, 'a useful stone is never a weight.'

U

Walking Companions

Nasrudin was returning from a visit to his in-laws in the country when he met the town Imam. Reluctant to walk alone, the Imam decided to suppress his dislike for the Mulla and join him on the way back to town. The two men had not been walking long when the road began to climb steeply, and the Imam could not resist a dig at his companion:

'Merciful Allah, you have certainly steepened this path to reward the Mulla for his irreligious thoughts.'

'Great Imam,' puffed Nasrudin, 'you are wasting valuable breath, for your observations are ill-conceived.'

'What does a blasphemer such as yourself, know of the workings of God?' snapped the Imam.

'This morning, when I took this path on my outward journey, it sloped downwards and was easy to walk. It is only now that you have joined me that the steep rise has appeared.'

Wanted: a Foolish Man

Nasrudin was sent by the King to find the most foolish man in the land and bring him to the palace as Court jester. The Mulla travelled to each town and village, in turn, but could not find a man stupid enough for the job. Finally, he returned alone.

'Have you located the greatest idiot in our kingdom?' asked the Monarch.

'Yes,' replied Nasrudin, 'but he is too busy looking for fools to take the job.'

Warriors' Tales

'At the Battle of Bokhara,' boasted one warrior, 'my steed was felled, and my right arm was severed, but I managed to continue to mow down my foes with my left arm.'

'That is nothing!' declared a second knight. 'In the same battle an enemy warrior buried his axe in my skull and gouged out my eye, but I battled on and came home with his head on a pike.'

'Child's play!' replied Nasrudin, tiring of their boasts. 'In the very same battle, a rival, forty-six foot tall, drew his sword and swiped off my head. But such a warrior am I that I retrieved my head, placed it back on my shoulders, and carried on as if nothing had happened.'

What a Waste

Nasrudin passed a stall heaped high with tempting foods. There were piles of apricots and figs; great jars of pistachios, almonds and pine nuts; baskets full of eggs; bowls of cream, cheese and butter; and tray after tray of different sweets. Mulla Nasrudin noticed how the stall-keeper waited for customers and refilled the bowls, baskets and trays, without eating a single morsel from the tables.

'Are you minding the stall for the owner?' he enquired.

'What do you mean?' asked the merchant. 'I am the owner.'

'But how is it, then, that you don't eat?'

'I'm here to sell, not to eat.'

'What a waste,' replied Mulla. 'If this were my stall, I'd start with some dried fruit and nuts. Follow that with ten scrambled eggs. And have sweets for dessert.'

What Price Advice?

Nasrudin was hired by a merchant to carry a heavy crate to his mansion. When a fee of five gold pieces had been set, Nasrudin loaded the pack onto his shoulders and the two men started on their way. After several hours of trudging through treacherous mountain passes, the merchant turned to his porter.

'I have been thinking. Instead of offering you mere money, I would like to offer you something far more valuable: advice.'

Nasrudin was very annoyed by this blatant breach of contract, but decided to give the man the benefit of the doubt. Perhaps the advice would prove to be of great worth.

'Very well, what are your words of wisdom?'

'One, never believe a man who says he will show you the way to make a fortune overnight.'

'That seems fair,' thought Nasrudin, who had been burnt by such promises in the past.

'Two, never go on a journey, no matter how brief you intend it to be, without supplies of food and water sufficient for three days.'

'Another useful point,' agreed the Mulla.

'Three, always engage a man to do your dirty work who is stupid enough to trade money for worthless advice,' said the merchant with a bellow of mirth.

'Your advice has proved so valuable that I fear that I owe you some change,' replied Nasrudin, struggling to hide his fury at the trick.

'Never annoy a member of your work force who is doing a job that you yourself are incapable of doing.' With this, he dropped the crate with a loud crash, and strode back down the mountainside.

What's the Difference?

'*I* have a riddle for you, Mulla,' the baker said to Nasrudin one day. 'What is the difference between a shepherd and a doctor?'

'Easy,' replied Nasrudin. 'A shepherd kills and then fleeces, while a doctor fleeces and then kills.'

What to Do?

Nasrudin set off into town leading his donkey with his son in the saddle. 'Look at the old man!' sniggered a youth. 'He lets the boy ride, while he limps along beside.'

Stopping, Nasrudin lifted his son out of the saddle and climbed on the animal's back. They had not gone far when an old woman waved her fist:

'Shame on you! Making the little one walk when you ride.'

Stopping again, Nasrudin lifted his son on to the saddle behind him. A few metres on, another passer-by accosted him.

'That poor beast! Two on his back, and his legs buckling underneath him!'

Nasrudin and his son both got off the donkey and continued on their way. Minutes later, someone else called out:

'I see you are taking your pet for a walk, Mulla!'

Losing patience, Nasrudin dropped the reins and gave the donkey a sharp slap on the rump.

'Go and find an owner who knows what to do with you!' he shouted and, putting his son on his shoulders, he strode off.

When You See Me...

An honest trader from Nasrudin's town was preparing to leave on a long journey. Worried that thieves might break into his house in his absence, he took his savings to the money-lender and asked him to keep them in his safe. Many months later, the trader returned from his travels and went to retrieve his money from the money-lender.

'You are mistaken,' said the man, 'you left nothing with me.'

The trader argued for many hours, but the trickster refused to return his savings. In desperation, the man turned to Nasrudin.

When he had explained the situation, the Mulla said:

'I can help you, but you have to do exactly as I say. Tomorrow I will pass you in the town square. When you see me, say nothing.'

The trader was confused, but agreed to do exactly as Nasrudin asked.

Next day, he was sitting in the centre of town when Nasrudin, dressed in a bejewelled uniform, with knives and daggers hanging from his belt and a rifle slung across his back, rode past on a magnificent charger. He waited until a crowd had gathered, and then greeted the trader:

'It is good to see you again, brother. I trust that your

travels were as successful as my own expeditions. You must come to see the booty I have wrenched from my vanquished foes.'

Remembering his orders, the trader bowed low, but said nothing. It was not long before the money-lender hurried up.

'Your brother must be the strongest warrior in the land! Please do me the honour of coming to supper this evening. I have been meaning to return your savings to you. I kept them in my safe and would now like to repay them with interest.'

Where Does It Hurt?

Nasrudin was standing in for the muezzin when he slipped and fell from the minaret. Badly injured, he lay on the ground groaning.

'Where does it hurt?' asked the doctor, who had rushed to the wounded man.

'Climb to the top of the minaret and jump off, and you will be able to feel for yourself.'

Where There are People

One summer, while Nasrudin was at the Emir's Court, the city's inhabitants were pestered by flies. 'Is there no place free from the buzzing of these infernal insects?' shouted the Emir.

'There is one place, Majesty,' replied Nasrudin, 'but that place has no people.'

'And where is that?'

But Nasrudin would say no more than: 'Where there are no people there are no flies.'

The King was enraged by the Mulla's refusal to speak up, but decided to forget the incident for the time being.

Some weeks later, the King and his entourage set off to visit the ruler of another land. As the sun went down on the tenth day, the Emir ordered the caravan to halt and a camp was set up in the desert.

After the evening meal, the Emir asked Nasrudin to join him in order to discuss matters of the world. While the two were talking, a fly landed on the Emir's hand.

'You see!' he exclaimed. 'You say that where there are no people, there are no flies. But here, in the uninhabited desert, there are still flies.'

'Do you mean to say,' replied Nasrudin, 'that you are not a man?'

Where Will I Go?

'Nasrudin,' sighed the judge, 'when I leave this world, will I go to Heaven or Hell?'

'Heaven is too full of the innocent men whom you have sentenced to the gallows,' replied Nasrudin. 'But I hear they have reserved you a place of honour in Hell.'

W

Who Bought Whom?

asrudin was leading his new donkey home from market. Just outside town, a friend stopped him on the path.

'Did you go to the donkey auction?'

A little further on, another friend asked: 'What was the asking price?'

A hundred yards on, a third man stopped him. 'Did you haggle?'

Nasrudin became so tired by the questions that he removed the donkey's lead and attached it to his own neck and continued on his way.

A fourth man saw him. 'You've finally bought a new donkey then?'

'Actually,' replied the Mulla, 'the donkey bought me.'

Whom to Respect

'Tell me, Nasrudin,' asked the mayor, 'who are the men you most respect?'

'Those who invite me to join them at a table overflowing with delicacies,' replied the Mulla.

'You must come to supper!' beamed the mayor.

'Then, from tonight, you will have my respect,' said Nasrudin.

Whose Beard?

Nasrudin dreamt that he had Satan's beard in his hand. Tugging the hair he cried: 'The pain you feel is nothing compared to that which you inflict on the mortals you lead astray.' And he gave the beard such a tug that he woke up yelling in agony. Only then did he realise that the beard he held in his hand was his own.

Why Pay Twice?

*N*asrudin ate a meal at a restaurant and left without paying the bill. The owner chased after him.

'You can't leave without paying!'

'Did you buy the ingredients in the bazaar?' asked Nasrudin.

'Yes.'

'Then the food has already been paid for once. Why pay twice?'

Window Shopping

A hungry Mulla Nasrudin was once walking through the bazaar. Passing a kebab stall he stopped and watched the succulent meat being roasted.

'Those kebabs — are they from meat so fresh that the lamb was yesterday grazing on the hillside?'

'Yes, this is the freshest meat you are likely to find in the whole town.'

'And do you take this tender meat, add spices and then roast it over the flames until cooked to perfection?'

'Yes! Yes!'

'And is it so exquisite that tears of pleasure come to the eyes of any man who eats it?'

'Brother,' intoned the stallholder, 'until you try these kebabs you have not lived!'

'What a shame it is, then,' replied Nasrudin, 'that I am only window shopping.'

Winter Coat

*N*asrudin's wife had finally finished making a grand winter coat for her husband. The Mulla, very pleased by its rich cloth and elegant style, wound an enormous turban around his head to complement the garment. He then left for town in order to show off his new attire. He hadn't gone more than a few paces when a stranger approached him and handed him a piece of paper.

'I have just received this letter and would be grateful if you could read it to me, as it is written in Arabic and I am unfamiliar with the language.'

Confused, Nasrudin returned the letter. 'I'm afraid I don't know Arabic either.'

'But you are dressed as an Arab, surely you speak your native tongue.'

The Mulla carefully removed his turban and coat and put them on the man.

'Now that you are an Arab, you can read the letter yourself!'

W

Wise Investment

'*I* am now old enough to be trusted with adult responsibilities,' the young Nasrudin told his father.

'If you are old enough to be trusted, take your mother's earrings to be mended.'

Nasrudin took the earrings straight to the bazaar and sold them — pocketing the money.

'The jeweller says the earrings will take a few days to repair,' he told his father. Delighted by the youth's seemingly trustworthy nature, Nasrudin's father gave him three weeks' pocket money in advance.

'Take this money and invest it wisely.'

Nasrudin ran off to the nearest sweet-shop and spent all the money on sweets, which he quickly consumed.

Three weeks later his father asked how he had invested his money.

'I'm glad you ask,' replied Nasrudin. 'I had thought of investing in silver, but am relieved to say that I bought chocolate instead.'

'Wretched boy! And to think I believed you were responsible.'

'But father, if I had invested in silver, who is to say that it, too, wouldn't have melted in the sun and trickled away just like mother's earrings?'

With One Silver Piece

Nasrudin tossed and turned the whole night, troubled by a vivid nightmare. In the dream, he found himself cooking a pot of grass over an open fire. Next morning, he described the scene to his wife:

'That sounds like an omen of some sort,' she said. 'You'd better find someone to explain its significance.'

Nasrudin hurried off to the fortune-teller, to whom he recounted the nightmare.

'You are quite right to enlist my help,' replied the crone. 'Cross my palm with silver and I will explain all.'

'If I had any silver,' snapped the Mulla, 'I could afford some decent food, and wouldn't be forced to cook grass!'

Woken the Wrong Man

While on his travels, Nasrudin teamed up with two other men.

One night, the three — a trader, a dervish, and Nasrudin — agreed to share a room at a hotel. They had decided to part company the next day, as their paths no longer ran in the same direction. Wanting to make an early start, Nasrudin tipped the hotelier to wake him before dawn.

Next morning, he struggled into his clothes and left the room while the other men continued to snore. Several hours later, the Mulla found a river and went to the water to drink. Seeing the dervish's coat and hat reflected in the water, he cursed:

'Damn that fool of a hotelier. He has woken up the wrong man!'

Women of Distant Lands

A general once came to Nasrudin's town in order to recruit men into the army.

'Any soldier serving our powerful Emperor may carry away the women of our enemies. In one land, for example, the maidens have plaits of raven-black hair down to their ankles.'

'How long are their legs?' asked the village wit.

'Their legs…' blustered the veteran, 'are as long as their beautiful locks.'

'I hope each man in your army is issued with a ladder,' said Nasrudin.

Worth Stealing

'Nasrudin!' whispered his wife in the middle of the night. 'Wake up! There are thieves in the house!'

'Keep quiet!' replied her husband. 'I have already heard them. Perhaps they will find something worth stealing here and I will be able to surprise them and snatch it away.'

Worthy Men

While on his travels, Nasrudin was stopped in the bazaar and told by palace guards to make his way to the Court. Arriving in the resplendent throne-room, he was told to join a collection of the poor in order to hear the religious speeches of some of the city's most venerated holy men.

One by one, the notables — each dressed in finery more glittering than the last — addressed the audience. Their sermons, packed with spiritual sentiments designed to uplift even the most doubtful souls, lasted quite some time. As night fell, the King stood up.

'You,' he said, pointing to Mulla Nasrudin, 'tell us: Which of these spiritual leaders is most worthy of our emulation?'

'He,' replied Nasrudin, 'who, seeing that a pauper does not have enough to feed or clothe himself, does not offer salvation for a fee.'

Worthy of Cream

One day, Nasrudin's wife sent her young son out to the bazaar for some milk. Seeing the lad rush by with his pail, the Emir decided to have some fun: 'Where are you off to in such a hurry?' he called down to the street.

'To buy some milk,' replied the boy.

'Why buy what you can have for free? Give your pail to the guards and I will fill it myself.' But, as soon as he had the pail, he filled it with stagnant water and sent the boy on his way.

When Nasrudin heard of the Emir's joke, he resolved to get even. Some days later, hearing that the ruler was suffering from migraine, he scooped up a pail of dung and hurried to the palace.

'Great Emir,' he said to the groaning man, 'I have here a poultice which, applied to the scalp three times a day, will banish even the severest pain.'

The Emir was only too happy to apply the paste. But, on the third day, he could no longer stand the stench and called Nasrudin.

'What is this infernal remedy made of?'

'Usually, it is made of milk,' replied Nasrudin, 'but I naturally considered your Eminence worthy of cream.'

You Lost it, You Find it

Chopping wood in the forest, Nasrudin became very hot. He removed his coat and hung it over his donkey's back. He then returned to his chopping and, while his back was turned, a thief ran off with his coat. When he had enough logs, Nasrudin started to load the wood onto the donkey and realised that his coat had gone. Slapping the animal on the rump, he roared:

'You careless fool! Go and find the coat you lost and don't you dare to return without it!'

Y

You Must be Deaf

As muezzin, Nasrudin was responsible for calling the faithful to prayer. One day, when he was halfway through, the Imam shouted up to him: 'No one can hear you! Call louder!'

'How strange,' hollered Nasrudin, 'I can hear my voice three miles away!'

Y